Wilderness Navigation

mountaineers
outdoor
basics

Wilderness Navigation

Finding Your Way
Using Map, Compass,
Altimeter, & GPS

SECOND EDITION

Bob Burns
Mike Burns

THE MOUNTAINEERS BOOKS

*T*his book is dedicated to the memories of the teachers of navigation who have gone before us, including Clinton M. Kelley, Richard B. Kaylor, Erhard Wichert, and Scott Fischer. Without their knowledge and leadership some of us would still be lost in the wilderness.

THE MOUNTAINEERS BOOKS
is the nonprofit publishing arm of The Mountaineers Club,
an organization founded in 1906 and dedicated to the exploration,
preservation, and enjoyment of outdoor and wilderness areas.

1001 SW Klickitat Way, Suite 201, Seattle, WA 98134

First edition 1999. Second edition: first printing 2004, second printing 2005.

Published simultaneously in Great Britain by Cordee, 3a DeMontfort Street, Leicester, England, LE1 7HD

Manufactured in Canada

Project Editor: Laura Drury
Copy Editor: Joeth Zucco
Cover and Book Design: The Mountaineers Books
Layout Artist: Kristy L. Welch
Illustrators: J. Schontz. Illustrations on pages 20, 21, 28, 31, 32, 35, 36, 37, 38, 40, 41, 48, 49, 51, 55, 56, 57, 58, 93, 103, 117 are from Mountaineering: The Freedom of the Hills, 7th ed. Seattle: The Mountaineers Books, 2003. Cox, Steven M., and Kris Fulsaas, eds.
Cover photograph: Nancy Duncan-Cashman

Library of Congress Cataloging-in-Publication Data
Burns, Bob, 1942-
  Wilderness navigation : finding your way using map, compass, altimeter & GPS / Bob Burns and Mike Burns.— 2nd ed.
      p. cm.
  Includes bibliographical references and index.
  ISBN 0-89886-953-6 (pbk.)
  1. Orienteering—Equipment and supplies. 2. Navigation—Equipment and supplies. 3. Outdoor recreation—Equipment and supplies. I. Burns, Mike, 1970- II. Title.
  GV200.4.B87 2004
  796.58—dc22

                    2004003366

Contents

Preface and Acknowledgments   8

Introduction   10

1. MAP BASICS   13
    USGS Topographic Maps   14
    How to Read Topographic Maps   15
    Limitations of Maps   23
    Customizing and Modifying Maps   24
    Carrying Maps on a Wilderness Trip   24
    Where to Get Maps   25
    The Importance of the Map   26

2. COMPASS BASICS   27
    Types of Base Plate Compasses   29
    Bearings   30
    Bearings in the Field   31
    Magnetic Declination   34
    Back Bearings   38
    Bearings on the Map   39
    Practicing with the Compass   41
    Tips on Compass Use   42
    The Map and Compass: A Checklist   43
    And for the Last Time   45

3. ORIENTATION WITH MAP AND COMPASS   46
    Point Position   47
    Line Position   47
    Area Position   48
    Orienting a Map   50
    Direction and Bearing of the Slope   51
    A Reminder   53

4. NAVIGATION WITH MAP AND COMPASS   54

Map and Compass   54
Compass Alone   56
Using Intermediate Objectives   56
The Intentional Offset ("Aiming Off")   57
The Parallel Path   58
Navigating around an Obstruction   59
Always Know Where You Are Headed, and Consider the Return
   Route   60
A Reminder   61

5. LOST!   62

How to Avoid Getting Lost   62
What If You Do Get Lost?   68

6. MORE ABOUT MAPS   71

Distance Measurement on the Map   71
Slope Measurement on the Map   74
Range, Township, and Section   77

7. MORE ABOUT COMPASSES AND GEOMAGNETISM   81

Where to Get Declination Information   81
Changes in Declination   82
Dip   86
Using the Clinometer   87
Other Types of Compasses   88

8. THE ALTIMETER   92

What the Altimeter Is and How It Works   92
Types of Altimeters   92
Effects of Weather on Altimeters   93
Precision and Accuracy   94
Effects of Temperature on Altimeters   94
Cautions When Using the Altimeter in Wilderness Travel   94
Orientation   94
Navigation   95
Decision Making   95
Use of Bearing of the Slope with the Altimeter   96

9. THE GLOBAL POSITIONING SYSTEM   97

Selecting a GPS Receiver   97
Getting Started with GPS   98

Using a GPS Receiver in Wilderness Navigation 99
Orientation Using GPS and UTM Coordinates 101
Navigation Using GPS and UTM Coordinates 104
Datums, Zones, and Bands 105
Limitations of GPS Receivers 106

10. WILDERNESS ROUTEFINDING 109
On the Trail 110
In the Forest 111
In Alpine Areas 113
On Snow 114
Wands 116
On Glaciers 118
Moats and Bergschrunds 120
The Bootprint 121
The Art of Wilderness Routefinding 122

Bibliography 124

Appendix: Wilderness Navigation Practice Problems 127

Index 138

Preface and Acknowledgments

The origins of this book are lost among the rough notes of The Mountaineers's first climbing course held in 1934. They were eventually published in 1960 as *Mountaineering: The Freedom of the Hills*, a comprehensive mountain climbing book, containing information on equipment, navigation, wilderness travel, and technical details of climbing on rock, snow, and glaciers. It has been revised six times since its initial publication, and we have contributed to several of the past revisions.

In addition to writing about navigation, we have hiked, scrambled, snowshoed, and climbed extensively as well as taught navigation in courses sponsored by The Mountaineers. In some of the non-climbing classes we were often asked to recommend a book covering the material presented in our courses and lectures. However, the only book using the same methods and covering the same material as these courses was *Freedom of the Hills*. Some skiers, snowshoers, and hikers balked at buying a large book filled with details of technical rock and ice climbing just to obtain information on navigation; it was out of this need that the idea for *Wilderness Navigation* emerged.

Wilderness Navigation was originally envisioned as a small, affordable book containing the same information covered in the navigation chapter of *Freedom of the Hills*. However, a lot of useful information had been excluded from *Freedom of the Hills* in order to keep its size manageable. *Wilderness Navigation* was therefore expanded with the addition of considerable technical information as well as material on wilderness routefinding and an appendix with thirty practice problems. The goal was surpassed, as it provided more than twice as much material as the navigation chapter in *Freedom of the Hills*.

The methods of using maps and compasses in this book have been taught for many years by The Mountaineers. When using the methods explained in this book, orienting the map is not necessary, nor is it necessary to add or subtract declination, or to draw declination lines on your maps. Instead, we explain how to make all compasses work like compasses with adjustable declination. This has proven to be an easy and dependable method of dealing with declination.

Since the original publication of *Wilderness Navigation* in 1999, we have received a number of suggestions for improvement from readers. We have incorporated many of these suggestions in this second edition, including the addition of the section-range-township method of land surveying, an update to the descriptions of compasses and Global Positioning System (GPS) receivers available, and updated declination maps for the United States and the world. Since 1999, there have also been some important changes to the GPS, requiring updates to that chapter. We have added more information on navigational techniques, as well as websites and other computer sources containing useful navigational information. The map and compass chapters have been split into two chapters each: Map Basics (chapter 1) and More about Maps (chapter 6), and Compass Basics (chapter 2) and More about Compasses and Geomagnetism (chapter 7). The intent of this change is to allow the reader to become thoroughly proficient in the essentials of map and compass use without getting bogged down in refined techniques that are not required for a basic understanding of navigation.

ACKNOWLEDGMENTS

We wish to express our appreciation to a number of individuals who have contributed to this book. Thanks to Larry Newitt and the Geological Survey of Canada, who created the Canadian Geomagnetic Reference Field that we used to create the declination map of the United States. We are grateful to our friend Ronald Gailis for his research into sources of information on geomagnetism, and to Jeff Renner for providing review and input on the subjects of the altimeter and weather. Thanks also to Jim Giblin for his assistance with photography, and to John Bell for providing some perspectives on the use of the GPS.

We also thank the staff of The Mountaineers Books, particularly Margaret Foster and Deb Easter, for bringing our vision to life. Finally, a thank you to the Navigation Committee of The Mountaineers and its first chairman Morgan Robinson for helpful suggestions and for adopting our book for use in The Mountaineers's navigation course.

Introduction

Where am I? How far is it to my destination? Will I be able to find my way back? These are some of the most frequently asked questions in wilderness travel, and this book shows you how to find the answers by using orientation and navigation.

By the time you finish reading this book, you will have a good handle on the tools of navigation and the proven techniques of top-notch navigators, who have acquired their skills through years of roaming—and being lost in—the wilderness. You will have the basic knowledge to head into the wilds, work out the way to your destination, and, most importantly, find your way home.

The tools and techniques are simple and straightforward—but exacting. Study them carefully to help make your wilderness adventures successful and to keep you safe and within the ranks of surviving navigators. Before you immerse yourself in this book, remember two things: navigation is easy and navigation is fun. (So much fun, in fact, that some people engage in the sport of *orienteering*, in which the participants compete with one another using map and compass to get to various destinations on a structured course.)

First, a few definitions:

Orientation is the science of determining your exact position on the earth. People who spend a reasonable amount of time and effort usually gain these skills, even if they have little background or interest in math or science.

Navigation is the science of determining the location of your objective and keeping yourself pointed in the right direction from your starting point to this destination. Like orientation, navigation is a required skill for all wilderness travelers.

Routefinding is the art of selecting and following the best path appropriate for the abilities and equipment of the party. It takes a lot to be a good routefinder: an integrated sense of terrain, as well as a combination of good judgment, experience, acute awareness, and instinct. In addition to a solid foundation in the orientation and navigation skills described in the following chapters, wilderness routefinding also requires considerable time, practice, and experience.

The route through this book is divided into two parts. The first, consisting of chapters 1 through 5, contains information on maps, compasses, orientation, navigation, how to avoid getting lost, and what to do if you *do* get lost. To become adept at using a map and compass, these chapters are essential to all outdoor travelers: hikers, scramblers, skiers, snowshoers, mountain climbers, and any other sporting enthusiasts who venture off the road and into the wilderness, including those who never intend to leave a well-maintained trail.

Chapters 6 through 10 provide more detailed information on the use of maps and compasses; the use of clinometers, altimeters, and GPS receivers; and wilderness routefinding on trails, in the forest, in alpine areas, and on snow and glaciers. We recommend a careful reading of these chapters for anyone who intends to leave the trail and venture cross-country in search of hidden fishing lakes, challenging mountain peaks, interesting cross-country ski routes, and other destinations beyond the well-maintained trail.

If you do not already have a compass, we suggest that you read chapter 2 before buying one.

This book will *not* make you an expert in wilderness navigation; only practice and experience will. But this book *can* give you a basic foundation in the skills necessary for safe and enjoyable wilderness travel.

Remember: this is a book about *orientation, navigation,* and *routefinding.* It is *not* a book about how to climb steep snow, travel safely in avalanche-prone areas, climb technical rock, or travel in safety on glaciers. Doing any of these activities requires that the traveler take courses and have considerable practice in the necessary techniques, under the tutelage of experienced and qualified individuals or groups. The bibliography at the end of this book suggests some resources covering these subjects. We urge you to study and practice such subjects carefully before undertaking any potentially hazardous travel.

A NOTE ABOUT SAFETY

Safety is an important concern in all outdoor activities. No book can alert you to every hazard or anticipate the limitations of every reader. The descriptions of techniques and procedures in this book are intended to provide general information. This is not a complete text on wilderness travel. Nothing substitutes for formal instruction, routine practice, and plenty of experience. When you follow any of the procedures described here, you assume responsibility for your own safety. Use this book as a general guide to further information. Under normal conditions, excursions into the backcountry require attention to traffic, road and trail conditions, weather, terrain, the capabilities of your party, and other factors. Keeping informed on current conditions and exercising common sense are the keys to a safe, enjoyable outing.

The Mountaineers Books

Map Basics

A map is a symbolic picture of a place. In convenient shorthand, it conveys a phenomenal amount of information in a form that is easy to understand and easy to carry. No one should venture into the wilderness without a map of the area, or without the skills required to interpret and thoroughly understand it.

You can find a lot of useful information on a map. The most important for wilderness travelers is topographic features, vegetation, and elevation information, which are discussed in this chapter. (See chapter 6 for more in-depth information, such as distance and slope measurement and surveying information on maps.) Note the publication date of the map and try to obtain the latest information because roads, trails, and other features may have changed. Several different types of maps are available:

Relief maps attempt to show terrain in three dimensions by using various shades of green, gray, and brown, terrain sketching, and raised surfaces. They help in visualizing the ups and downs of the landscape and have some value in trip planning.

Land management and recreation maps are frequently updated and thus are very useful for current details on roads, trails, ranger stations, and other works of the human hand. They usually show only the horizontal relationship of natural features, without the contour lines that indicate the shape of the land. These maps, published by the U.S. Forest Service, National Park Service, other government agencies, and timber companies, are often quite helpful for trip planning.

Sketch maps tend to be crudely drawn but often make up in specialized route detail what they lack in draftsmanship. Such drawings can be effective supplements to other map and guidebook information.

Guidebook maps vary greatly in quality. Some are merely sketches, while others are accurate modifications of topographic maps. They often contain useful details on roads, trails, and wilderness routes.

Topographic maps are the best of all for wilderness travelers. They depict topography, the shape of the earth's surface, by showing contour lines that represent constant elevations above and below sea level. These maps, essential to off-trail travel, are produced in many countries. Some are produced by government agencies, such as the U.S. Geological Survey (USGS), whereas others are printed by private companies. Some private companies produce maps based on USGS maps and update them with recent trail and road details, sometimes combining sections of different USGS maps into one. These maps are often useful supplements to standard topographic maps and are particularly useful in trail hiking. As an example of topographic maps, we will look in detail at USGS maps.

USGS TOPOGRAPHIC MAPS

It will be helpful to start this discussion of USGS maps with a description of how cartographers divide up the earth. The distance around our planet is divided into 360 units called *degrees*. A measurement east or west is called *longitude*. A measurement north or south is called *latitude*. Longitude is measured from 0° to 180°, both east and west, starting at the Greenwich meridian near London, England. Latitude is measured from 0° to 90°, north and south, from the equator. New York City, for example, is situated at 74 degrees west longitude and 41 degrees north latitude (74° W and 41° N).

Each degree is divided into sixty units called *minutes* (designated with a ' symbol), and each minute is further subdivided into sixty *seconds* (designated with a " symbol). On a map, a latitude of 46 degrees, 53 minutes, and 15 seconds north would be written like this: 46°53'15"N.

One type of USGS map commonly used by wilderness travelers covers an area of 7.5 minutes (that is, 1/8 degree) of latitude by 7.5 minutes of longitude. These maps are known as the *7.5-minute series*. An older type of USGS map covers an area of 15 minutes (that is, 1/4 degree) of latitude by 15 minutes of longitude. These maps are part of what is called the *15-minute series*.

The *scale* of a map is a ratio between measurements on the map and measurements in the real world. A common way to state the scale is to compare a map measurement with a ground measurement (as in 1 inch equals 1 mile) or to give a specific mathematical ratio (as in 1:24,000, where any one unit of measure on the map equals 24,000 units of the same measure on the earth). The scale is shown graphically, usually at the bottom of the map.

In the USGS 7.5-minute series, the scale is 1:24,000, or roughly 2.5 inches to the mile, or 4 centimeters (cm) to the kilometer (km). Each map covers an area of approximately 6 by 9 miles (9 by 14 km). In the 15-minute series, the scale is 1:62,500, or about 1 inch to 1 mile (1.6 cm to 1 km), and each map covers an area of about 12 by 18 miles (18 by 28 km). Off-trail travelers prefer the 7.5-minute maps because of the greater detail.

The 7.5-minute map is the standard for the continental United States and Hawaii. The 15-minute map is the standard only for Alaska; the scale is 1:63,360, or exactly 1 inch to 1 mile. The north-south extent of each Alaska map is 15 minutes but the east-west extent is greater than 15 minutes, because of the way in which the lines of longitude converge toward the North Pole.

HOW TO READ TOPOGRAPHIC MAPS

A map's language is easy to learn and pays immediate rewards to any wilderness traveler. Some of this language is in words, but most of it is in the form of symbols. Each map is referred to as a quadrangle (or quad) and covers an area bounded on the north and south by latitude lines that differ by an amount equal to the map series (7.5 minutes or 15 minutes), and on the east and west by longitude lines that differ by the same amount, except for Alaska. Each quadrangle is given the name of a prominent feature in the area.

Declination Information and North-South Reference Lines

The margins of USGS maps contain important information, such as the date of publication and revision, the names of maps of adjacent areas, contour intervals, and map scales. The margin also gives the area's magnetic declination, which is the difference between true north and magnetic north. Declination is extremely important and will be discussed in chapter 2. USGS topographic maps printed in 1988 or later (see fig. 1a) have a statement such as "1990 Magnetic North Declination 20° EAST." Maps printed before 1988 usually have a declination diagram printed near the lower left-hand corner (see fig. 1b). The star indicates true north and the "MN" indicates magnetic north. The difference between these two is the magnetic declination.

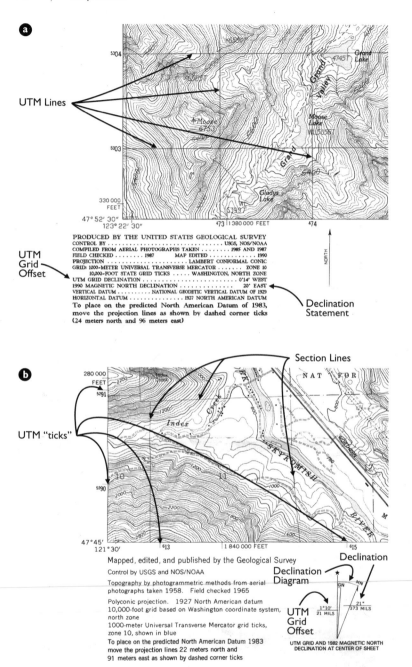

a

UTM Lines

UTM Grid Offset

PRODUCED BY THE UNITED STATES GEOLOGICAL SURVEY
CONTROL BY . . . . USGS, NOS/NOAA
COMPILED FROM AERIAL PHOTOGRAPHS TAKEN . . . . 1985 AND 1987
FIELD CHECKED 1987   MAP EDITED 1990
PROJECTION . . . . LAMBERT CONFORMAL CONIC
GRID: 1000-METER UNIVERSAL TRANSVERSE MERCATOR . . . . . . ZONE 10
10,000-FOOT STATE GRID TICKS . . . . . WASHINGTON, NORTH ZONE
UTM GRID DECLINATION . . . . 0°14′ WEST
1990 MAGNETIC NORTH DECLINATION . . . . 20′ EAST
VERTICAL DATUM . . . . NATIONAL GEODETIC VERTICAL DATUM OF 1929
HORIZONTAL DATUM . . . . 1927 NORTH AMERICAN DATUM
To place on the predicted North American Datum of 1983,
move the projection lines as shown by dashed corner ticks
(24 meters north and 96 meters east)

Declination Statement

b

Section Lines

UTM "ticks"

Mapped, edited, and published by the Geological Survey

Control by USGS and NOS/NOAA

Topography by photogrammetric methods from aerial
photographs taken 1958.   Field checked 1965

Polyconic projection.   1927 North American datum
10,000-foot grid based on Washington coordinate system,
north zone
1000-meter Universal Transverse Mercator grid ticks,
zone 10, shown in blue

To place on the predicted North American Datum 1983
move the projection lines 22 meters north and
91 meters east as shown by dashed corner ticks

Declination Diagram

Declination

UTM Grid Offset

GN   MN

1°10′
21 MILS

21°
373 MILS

UTM GRID AND 1982 MAGNETIC NORTH
DECLINATION AT CENTER OF SHEET

Figure 1. Lower left corner of USGS topographic maps: a. newer than 1988, b. older than 1988

Depending on the map's date of revision, there may or may not be Universal Transverse Mercator (UTM) lines printed on the map. Maps printed in 1988 or later usually have a grid of black lines representing the 1000-meter intervals of the UTM grid (see fig. 1a). This grid is usually slightly offset from true north. The amount of this offset is given by a statement in the lower left corner of the map such as "UTM GRID DECLINATION 0°14' WEST." The UTM grid is very helpful when using a global positioning system (GPS) receiver (see chapter 9). These lines may also be used as a north-south reference (see chapter 2), but only if the offset of the grid is less than 1°. If the offset of the UTM grid is more than 1°, then you should use surveyors' section lines (usually printed in red). If the map has no section lines, or if the section lines do not truly run north-south, then you should draw in your own north-south lines. Put your map on a table and place one long edge of a yardstick along the left margin of the map. Draw a line along the other side of the yardstick, and then move the yardstick over to the line you have just drawn and draw another line, and another, and so on until you reach the center of the map. Then place the yardstick along the right margin of the map and repeat the procedure. This way, you will have a set of north-south lines that are truly north-south. This will help you achieve accuracy in measuring and plotting bearings on the map using your compass (see chapter 2).

On maps printed prior to 1988, UTM lines are usually not shown. However, there are faint tick marks along the edges of such maps showing the locations of the 1000-meter lines (see fig. 1b). The declination diagrams for these maps usually have a line to "GN," meaning grid north. This is the offset of the UTM grid from true north. If this offset is less than 1°, then you can connect these tick marks on your table at home using a yardstick to place a UTM grid on the map. You can then use these as north-south reference lines. However, if the amount of difference between true north and grid north is greater than 1°, then you should draw in your own north-south lines parallel with the edges of the map, as described above.

What the Colors Mean

Colors on a USGS topographic map have specific meanings:

Red: Major roads and survey information.

Blue: Rivers, lakes, springs, waterfalls, and other water features.

Black: Minor roads, trails, railroads, buildings, bench marks, latitude and longitude lines, UTM coordinates and lines, and other features not part of the natural environment.

Green: Areas of heavy forest. Solid green marks a forested area, while mottled green indicates scrub vegetation. A lack of green does not mean that an area is devoid of vegetation but simply that any growth is too small or scattered to show on the map. You should not be surprised if a small, narrow gully with no green color on the map turns out to be an avalanche gully, choked with impassable brush in the summer and fall and posing a significant avalanche hazard in the winter and spring.

White: The color of the paper on which the map is printed; it can have a variety of meanings, depending on the terrain.

White with blue contour lines: A glacier or permanent snowfield. The contour lines of glaciers and permanent snowfields are in solid blue, with their edges indicated by dashed blue lines. Elevations are shown in blue. Rope up for all glacier travel!

White with brown contour lines: Any other area without substantial forest, such as a high alpine area, a clear-cut, a rock slide, an avalanche gully, or a meadow. Study the map for other clues.

Brown: Contour lines and elevations, everywhere except on glaciers and permanent snowfields.

Purple: Partial revision of an existing map.

Translating Contour Lines

The heart of a topographic map is its overlay of contour lines, each line indicating a constant elevation as it follows the shape of the landscape. A map's contour interval is the difference in elevation between two adjacent contour lines. The contour interval is clearly printed at the bottom of the map. Every fifth contour line, called an *index contour,* is printed darker than the other lines and is labeled with the elevation.

For practice in identifying elevations on a map, see problems 4 and 12 in the appendix.

One of the most important bits of information a topographic map reveals is whether you will be traveling uphill or downhill. If the route crosses lines of increasingly higher elevation, you will be going uphill. If it crosses lines of decreasing elevation, the route is downhill. Flat or sidehill travel is indicated by a route that crosses no lines and remains within a single contour interval.

Topographic maps also show cliffs, passes, summits, and other features (fig. 2). Main features depicted by contour lines include the following:

Flat areas: No contour lines at all.

Gentle slopes: Widely spaced contour lines.

Steep slopes: Closely spaced contour lines.

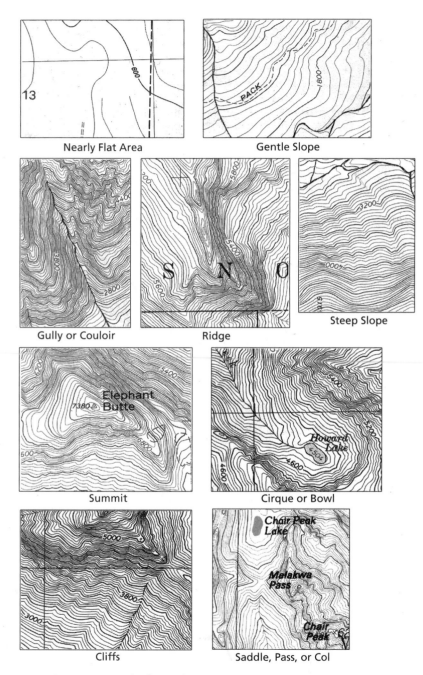

Figure 2. Basic topographic features

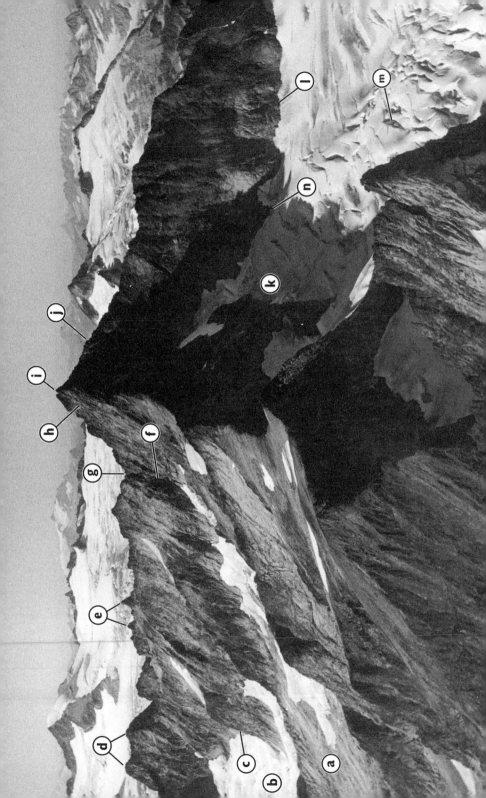

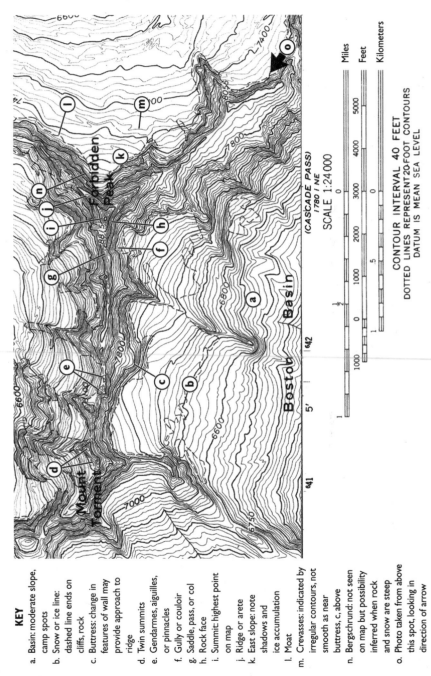

KEY

a. Basin: moderate slope, camp spots
b. Snow or ice line: dashed line ends on cliffs, rock
c. Buttress: change in features of wall may provide approach to ridge
d. Twin summits
e. Gendarmes, aiguilles, or pinnacles
f. Gully or couloir
g. Saddle, pass, or col
h. Rock face
i. Summit: highest point on map
j. Ridge or arete
k. East slope: note shadows and ice accumulation
l. Moat
m. Crevasses: indicated by irregular contours, not smooth as near buttress, c, above
n. Bergschrund: not seen on map but possibility inferred when rock and snow are steep
o. Photo taken from above this spot, looking in direction of arrow

(CASCADE PASS)
1780 I NE
SCALE 1:24 000

CONTOUR INTERVAL 40 FEET
DOTTED LINES REPRESENT 20-FOOT CONTOURS
DATUM IS MEAN SEA LEVEL

Figure 3. Photograph of a mountainous area; keyed features are represented on the accompanying topographic map

Cliffs: Contour lines extremely close together or touching.

Valleys, ravines, gullies, and couloirs: Contour lines in a pattern of Us for gentle, rounded valleys or gullies; Vs for sharp valleys and gullies. The Us and Vs point uphill, in the direction of higher elevation.

Ridges or spurs: Contour lines in a pattern of Us for gentle, rounded ridges; Vs for sharp ridges. The Us and Vs point downhill, in the direction of lower elevation.

Peaks or summits: A concentric pattern of contour lines, with the summit being the innermost and highest ring. Peaks are also often indicated by Xs, elevations, bench marks (BMs), or triangle symbols.

Cirques or bowls: Patterns of contour lines forming a semicircle (or as much as three-quarters of a circle), rising from a low spot in the center to form a natural amphitheater at the head of a valley.

Saddles, passes, or cols: An hourglass shape, with higher contour lines on two sides, indicating a low point on a ridge.

As you travel in the wilderness, frequently observe the terrain and its depiction on the map. Note all the topographic features—such as ridges, gullies, streams, and summits—as you pass them. This helps you to maintain a close estimate of exactly where you are and helps you to become an expert map reader. You will get better and better at interpreting these lines by comparing actual terrain with its representation on the map (see fig. 3). The goal is to be able to glance at a topographic map and have a sharp mental image of just what the place will look like.

For practice in identifying topographic features on a map, see problems 1, 9, and 22 in the appendix.

Direction of the Slope

Traveling along a contour line means traveling on a level route with no slope. Conversely, the direction perpendicular (at a right angle) to a contour line gives the direction of the slope—the direction directly uphill or downhill, sometimes called the *fall line*. You can easily find this direction on the map or in the field for any point on sloping terrain. This fact can be very useful in orientation, and we will refer to it in several places in this book. For example, in figure 4, point G has a slope that falls off to the southwest. Point H, on the other hand, has a slope falling off roughly to the east. We will be able to express this direction more precisely after we explain how to measure and plot bearings using the compass in chapter 2.

Using the direction of the slope cannot prove that you are at any

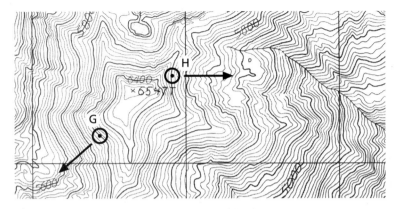

Figure 4. Examples of observing the direction of the slope on a map

particular place, but it can disprove it, and this can sometimes be a big help in trying to figure out where you are. In figure 4, for example, suppose you have climbed Peak 6547 and have descended a few hundred feet. You wish to find out where you are, and you guess that you are at point G. That means that the slope should be falling off to the southwest. However, when standing on the slope and facing downhill, you see the midday sun on your right, so you know that you are facing roughly east. This proves that you cannot be at point G. You could very possibly be at point H, since the slope there falls off to the east. But there are other places where the slope falls off to the east, so you cannot prove that you are at point H.

Problems 7 and 15 in the appendix provide practice in finding the direction of slope from a map.

LIMITATIONS OF MAPS

Keep a couple of cautionary thoughts in mind as you study a topographic map. The map will not show all the terrain features that you actually see on your trip because there is a limit to what mapmakers can jam onto the map without reducing it to an unreadable clutter. If a feature is not at least as high as the contour interval, it may not be shown, so a 30-foot cliff may come as a surprise when you are navigating with a map that has a 40-foot contour interval. Check the date of the map, because topographic maps are not revised very often, and information on forests and on roads and other works of the human hand could be out of date. A forest may have been logged or a road extended or closed since the last update. Although topographic maps are essential to wilderness travel, you often need to supplement them with information from visitors to the area, guidebooks, and other maps. When you learn of changes, you should note them on your map.

CUSTOMIZING AND MODIFYING MAPS

Sometimes a trip runs through portions of two or more maps. Adjoining maps can be folded at the edges and brought together, or you can create your own customized map by cutting out the non-pertinent areas and splicing the rest together with tape. Include plenty of territory so that you will have a good overview of the entire trip, including the surrounding area which might be needed for orientation (see chapter 3). Black-and-white photocopies are good for marking the route, but since they do not show colors, they should be used only as supplements to the real thing. If a durable, high-quality reproduction is needed, then a color photocopy onto waterproof paper may be the best approach. Some stores have the capability to produce computer-generated maps covering whatever area you want by combining various sections of USGS quadrangles. Though these customized maps are slightly more expensive than the standard USGS quadrangles, you may appreciate their convenience.

Some wilderness travelers cut off the white borders of their maps in order to minimize the amount of weight they carry. This practice is of questionable value, since these blank areas are useful for making notes regarding your trip, and the weight saved is minimal. If you do this, be careful not to cut off any of the very important information at the bottom of the map, such as the scales, date of the map, declination information, and contour interval. Some of the information at the lower left-hand corner of the map (see fig. 1) might not seem too important if you are not using the GPS (see chapter 9). But if you ever decide to buy a GPS receiver, you may later regret having cut off and discarded essential information regarding the UTM zone and map datum.

CARRYING MAPS ON A WILDERNESS TRIP

Taking into account the precious objects they are, maps deserve tender care in the wilds. You can make a map more durable by laminating it with a plastic film or by giving it a waterproof coating. Some maps can be purchased with a waterproof coating. Such coatings, however, are difficult to mark on and make the map harder to work with and fold. A waterproof coating also makes a map more slippery and more likely to slide down a snow slope if dropped.

Many people carry their maps in a well-protected place such as in the top flaps of their packs. In doing so, they protect their maps from the elements, but at the same time they make it inconvenient to look at them, since they must remove their packs to do so. Instead of doing this, we suggest that you carry your map in your pocket or some other readily accessible place so you do not have to take off your pack to get at it. Cargo shorts with big pockets are excellent for carrying maps, compasses, and other objects that you want to access quickly and conveniently. Elsewhere in this book, we will point out the importance of making frequent observations of the map to aid you in orientation and navigation. Following this advice is a lot easier if it is possible to get at your map at any time.

One good way to carry a map is to fold it to show the area where you will be traveling, and then enclose it in a clear plastic map case or a plastic zipper-lock bag. This way, it will be protected from the elements, always visible, easy to remove, and compact. If protected in this way, you can even glissade down a snow slope with the map in your back pocket without damaging it.

WHERE TO GET MAPS

Many outdoor recreation stores sell topographic maps; some bookstores and even some nautical supply stores stock them as well. Look in the yellow pages of the telephone directory under "Maps, retail."

Order maps directly from the USGS by calling 1-888-ASK-USGS, or writing USGS, 509 National Center, Reston, Virginia 20192. If you do not know the name of the map for the area you need, you can order a free *Topographic Map Index Circular* for your state as well as a booklet entitled *Topographic Maps*. The index circular shows the names of all the quadrangles in your state, so you can find which one(s) you need for any particular trip.

You can also order many topographic maps online from the USGS website at *www.usgs.gov*. From the homepage, follow the links to find and order a map. Many other useful maps, publications, and even aerial photographs are also available from this website. There are also links to many other websites of interest to people who want geographic data.

To obtain topographic maps for Canada, call 1-800-465-6277, or write to Canada Map Office, 615 Booth Street, Ottawa, Ontario K1A 0E9.

You can create your own topographic maps with software such as TOPO! and DeLorme's Topo USA, and from several Internet sites such as *www.topozone.com*. Keep in mind that your software-generated map will only be as good as allowed by your printer.

THE IMPORTANCE OF THE MAP

With the exception of your brain, the topographic map is your most important navigational tool. No one should venture into the wilderness without one. Maps give you information about direction, the distance between any two points, the shape of the terrain, human and natural features, the amount of vegetation, the location of water features, the direction and grade of the slope, and more. But as useful as maps are by themselves, they become even more powerful when used with a compass.

Compass Basics

The compass is a very simple device that can do a wondrous thing. It can reveal at any time and any place exactly what direction it is pointing. On a simple wilderness trek in good weather, the compass may never leave your pack or pocket. But as the route becomes more complex or as the weather worsens, it comes into its own as a critical tool of wilderness travel.

A compass is nothing more than a magnetized needle that responds to the earth's magnetic field. Compass makers have added a few things to this basic unit to make it easier to use. But stripped to the core, there is just that needle, aligned with the earth's magnetism, and from that we can figure out any direction.

The basic features (see fig. 5a) of a compass to be used for wilderness travel include:

▶ A freely rotating magnetic needle—one end is a different color (usually red) from the other so you can tell which end points to north.

▶ A circular, rotating housing, or capsule, for the needle—filled with a fluid that dampens (reduces) the vibrations of the needle, making readings more accurate.

▶ A dial around the circumference of the housing—graduated clockwise in 2-degree increments from 0° to 360°.

▶ An orienting arrow and a set of parallel meridian lines—located below the needle.

▶ An index line—used to set and read bearings.

▶ A transparent, rectangular base plate for the entire unit—includes a direction-of-travel line (sometimes with an arrow at

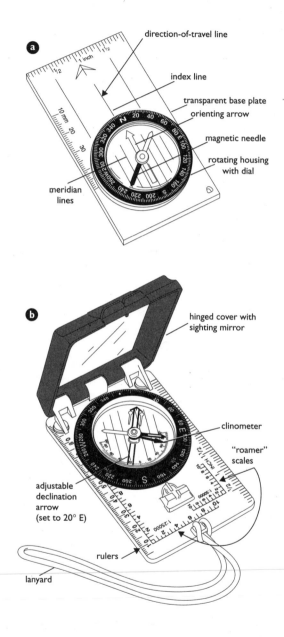

Figure 5. Features of compasses used in wilderness navigation: a. essential features, b. useful optional features

one end) to point toward your objective. The longer the base plate, the more accurate your reading will be.

Optional features (see fig. 5b) available on some compasses include:

▶ An adjustable declination arrow—an easy, dependable way to correct for magnetic declination; well worth the added cost.

▶ A sighting mirror—another way to improve accuracy.

▶ A ruler—calibrated in inches or millimeters; used to measure short distances on a map.

▶ A clinometer—used to measure the angle of a slope in the field.

▶ A magnifying glass—used to help read closely-spaced contour lines and other minute details on maps.

Some compasses have an adjustable declination arrow but no mirror. These cost a little more than the basic compass of figure 5a but considerably less than the full-featured compass of figure 5b. They offer a good compromise for someone who prefers the adjustable declination arrow but does not want to pay the added cost of the mirror.

Most compasses have a lanyard—a piece of string a foot or so long for attaching the compass to your belt, jacket, or pack. It is not a good idea to put the lanyard around your neck; this can be an unsafe practice, particularly when doing any technical climbing, difficult scrambling, or when climbing over and under fallen logs.

Small, round, cheap compasses without base plates are not accurate enough for wilderness travel, nor can you use them for working with a map. For routefinding, the compass must be accurate to within 2°. A larger error, say 5°, can land a party 700 meters off target at the end of an 8-kilometer trip, or 2300 feet in 5 miles of travel.

TYPES OF BASE PLATE COMPASSES

The base plate compasses listed here are the ones we know about as we go to press. By the time the book hits the streets, some of these may be discontinued, while still other good ones may appear. But this listing should at least give you an idea of what types of compasses are available.

Minimal compasses: (Approximately $10–$25) Silva Polaris Types 7 and 177, Explorer III Types 3 and 203; Nexus Expedition and Star 7DNL; Suunto A-10 Partner II and A40L. These meet all the basic requirements for wilderness travel but do not have features such as mirrors or declination corrections.

With mirror but no declination adjustment: (Approximately $15–$30) Nexus Safari, Pioneer, and Avalanche 26DNL-CL; Silva Guide Type 26 and Landmark 427; Suunto MCB Amphibian and MCA-D. Some people buy this type of compass, mistakenly assuming that since it has a mirror it must also have adjustable declination. This is not true. **With declination adjustment but no mirror:** (Approximately \$10–\$40) Suunto Locator M2-D, Leader M3-D, Contender M5-DL, Smoke Killer, and GPS Plotter; Brunton 8096 Eclipse GPS, 8097 Eclipse, and Classic 8010G and 9020G.

Full-featured: (Approximately \$30–\$90) Silva Ranger 15TDCL; Suunto MC-2 and MC-2 Global; Nexus Elite 15TDCL; Brunton 8040G, 8040 Elite, 8099 Eclipse, and 8099 Pro Eclipse. These top-of-the-line compasses have declination adjustment and mirrors, and some have clinometers. Though more expensive than the compasses described above, these are best for wilderness navigation.

Unacceptable compasses: Wrist and zipper-pull compasses. These have scales marked in 5-degree increments or do not have rectangular, transparent base plates.

If minimum cost is your primary concern, any of the minimal compasses will work, though you will need to make a slight modification to correct for magnetic declination, which will be described later.

If cost is not your primary factor, we strongly recommend any of the full-featured compasses.

And if you can afford a better compass than the minimal but do not wish to spend enough to get a full-featured model, then we recommend getting a compass with a declination adjustment but without a mirror or clinometer. Of all the optional features, the declination adjustment is the most useful.

The Silva, Suunto, and Nexus compasses mentioned above have meridian lines in the transparent base, as shown in figure 5. Several of the Brunton models mentioned above, such as the Classic 8010G, 9020G, and 8040, do not have meridian lines but can be used successfully in wilderness navigation using slightly different methods. In order to simplify our explanation of compass use, we will defer the discussion of those Brunton models until chapter 7. The rest of chapter 2 is therefore devoted to using compasses with meridian lines in the transparent base.

BEARINGS

A *bearing* is the direction from one place to another, measured in degrees of angle with respect to an accepted reference line. This reference is the line to true north.

The round dial of a compass is divided into 360 degrees. The direction in degrees to each of the cardinal directions, going clockwise around the dial starting from the top, is north, 0° (also 360°); east, 90°; south, 180°; and west, 270° (see fig. 6).

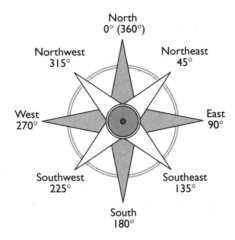

Figure 6. Cardinal directions and corresponding degrees on the compass

The compass is used for two basic tasks regarding bearings:
1. *To take, or measure, bearings.* To take a bearing means to measure the direction from one point to another, either on a map or in the field.
2. *To plot, or follow, bearings.* To plot a bearing means to set a certain bearing on the compass and then to plot out, or to follow, where that bearing points, either on the map or in the field.

BEARINGS IN THE FIELD

All bearings in the field are based on where the needle points. For the sake of simplicity, we will first ignore the effects of magnetic declination, a subject that will be taken up in the next section. Let us imagine that we are in Mississippi, where the declination is negligible.

To take (measure) a bearing in the field: Hold the compass in front of you and point the direction-of-travel line at the object whose bearing you want to find. Then rotate the compass housing until the pointed end of the orienting arrow is aligned with the north-seeking (usually red) end of the magnetic needle. (This process is sometimes referred to as "boxing the needle" or "getting the dog in the doghouse.") Read the bearing at the index line (fig. 7).

If the compass has no sighting mirror, hold it at or near arm's length and at or near waist level, with your arm straight at about a 45-degree angle from your body (see fig. 8). This is a compromise between sighting with the compass at eye level (sighting on your objective along the edge of the compass, without being able to see the compass

Last, read
bearing.

Second, align magnetic needle
with orienting arrow.

First,
sight
on
object.

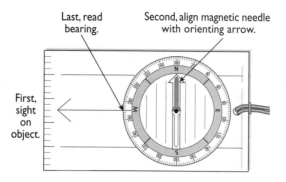

Figure 7. Taking a compass bearing in the field in an area with zero declination

Figure 8. Taking a bearing using a compass that does not have a mirror

Figure 9. Taking a bearing using a compass with a mirror

needle or orienting arrow) or holding it straight down (being able to see the compass needle and arrow without parallax but losing sight of the objective).

With a sighting mirror, no such compromise is necessary. Fold the mirror back to about a 45-degree angle and hold the compass at eye level, with the sight pointing at the object (see fig. 9). Observe the magnetic needle and the orienting arrow in the mirror as you rotate the housing to align the needle and the arrow. In either case, hold the compass level. Keep it away from metal objects, which can easily deflect the magnetic needle, giving you a false reading.

To follow (plot) a bearing in the field: Simply reverse the process you used to take a bearing. Rotate the compass housing until you have set the desired bearing at the index line, say 270° (west). Then hold the compass level in front of you, at roughly arm's length and waist height. Turn your entire body (including your feet) until the north-seeking end of the magnetic needle is aligned with the pointed end of the orienting arrow (i.e., box the needle). The direction of travel line is now pointing in whatever direction you have set at the index line, in this case west.

MAGNETIC DECLINATION

A compass needle is attracted to *magnetic* north, while most maps are printed with true north—the direction to the geographic north pole—at the top. This difference between the direction to true north and the direction to magnetic north, measured in degrees, is called *magnetic declination*. You will need to make a simple compass adjustment or modification to correct for declination.

Magnetic declination varies from place to place and over time. Always use the most current topographic map for your area. To find the amount and direction of declination for the map, look in the lower left corner on USGS topographic maps (see fig. 1). If the map is more than ten years old, the declination may be somewhat out of date. The amount of declination changes over time, by up to about 0.2° per year in some places in the United States. This means that declination can change up to 2° in a ten-year period of time in the United States. The map of the United States shown in figure 10 will give you a fairly good idea of the declination in your area. The map is for 2005 and is valid for the time interval from 2000 to 2010. (See chapter 7 for more information on determining the correct declination.)

In figure 10, you can see that the line of zero declination runs through parts of Minnesota, Wisconsin, Iowa, Illinois, Missouri, Arkansas, Mississippi, and Louisiana. Along this line, the magnetic needle points in the same direction as the geographic north pole (true north), so no correction for declination is necessary. But in areas west of this line, the magnetic needle points somewhere to the east (to the right) of true north, so these areas are said to have *east declination*. It works just the opposite on the other side of the line of zero declination, such as on the East Coast. Here, the magnetic needle points somewhere to the west (left) of true north, so these areas are said to have *west declination*.

Consider a wilderness traveler in Phoenix, Arizona, with a declination of 12° east. The true bearing is a measurement of the angle between the line to true north and the line to the objective, as shown in figure 11a. The magnetic needle, however, is pulled toward magnetic north, not true north. So instead it measures the angle between the line to magnetic north and the line to the objective. This "magnetic bearing" is 12° less than the true bearing. To get the true bearing, you could *add* 12° to the magnetic bearing.

As in Arizona, travelers in all areas west of the zero declination line could add the declination to the magnetic bearing to get a true bearing. In central Colorado, for example, about 10° would be added. In the central part of Washington state, it is about 18°.

East of the zero declination line, the declination can be *subtracted*

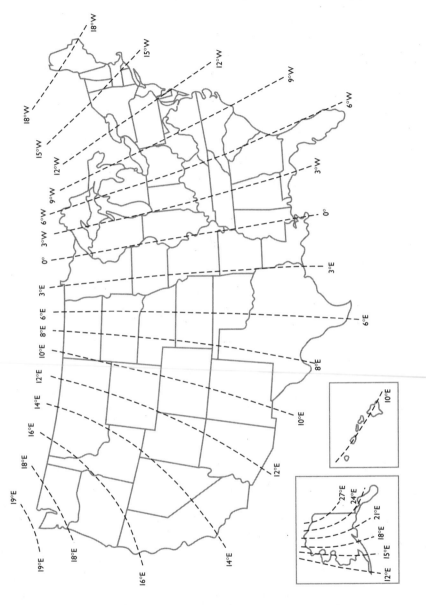

Figure 10. Magnetic declination in the United States in 2005

from the magnetic bearing to get the true bearing. In southern Vermont, for example (see fig. 11b), the magnetic bearing is about 15° greater than true bearing. To get a true bearing, the traveler in Vermont could subtract the declination of 15° from the magnetic bearing.

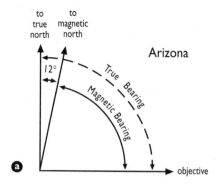

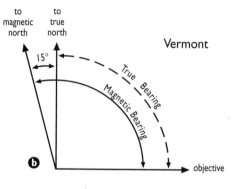

Figure 11. Magnetic and true bearings:
a. in Arizona (east declination),
b. in Vermont (west declination)

This is all very simple in theory but can be confusing in practice, and the wilderness is no place for mental arithmetic that can potentially have serious consequences. A more practical way to handle the minor complication of declination is to pay more for your compass and get one with an adjustable *declination arrow* instead of a fixed orienting arrow. By following the instructions supplied with the compass, you can easily set the declination arrow—usually by inserting a tiny screwdriver (often attached to the lanyard) into a small slot and turning it until the declination arrow points at the correct number of degrees east or west of the index line. Then the bearing that you read at the index line will automatically be the true bearing and concern about a declination error is one worry you can leave at home. Compasses with adjustable declination arrows are sometimes called "set and forget" compasses.

If you have a compass with adjustable declination and set it for a declination of 12° E, as for Phoenix, Arizona, then, once properly adjusted, the pointed end of the declination arrow will point to 12°. In southern Vermont, with a declination of 15° W, the correctly adjusted declination arrow will point to 345° (15° less than 360°).

On compasses without adjustable declination arrows, you can achieve the same effect by taping a thin, pointed strip of paper to the bottom of the rotating housing to serve as a customized declination arrow, as shown in figure 12.

In Arizona, your taped declination arrow must point at 12° east (clockwise) from the 360-degree point (marked *N* for north) on the rotating dial (fig. 12a). In Vermont, the declination arrow must point at 15° west (counterclockwise) from the 360-degree mark (fig. 12b),

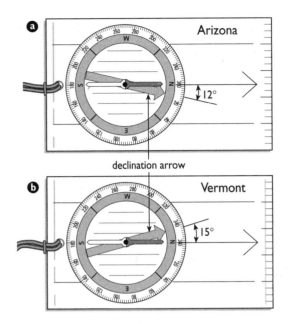

declination arrow

Figure 12.
Compass declination
corrections: a. for
an area west of the
zero-declination
line, b. for an area
east of the zero
declination line

or 345°. In the central part of Washington state, the declination arrow must point at 18° east (clockwise) from 360°. Note that this taped declination arrow is located exactly the same as the adjustable declination arrow described above.

If you travel to an area with different declination, you will have to change the declination correction. If you have a compass with an adjustable declination arrow, a minor screwdriver adjustment will allow you to set the compass for the new declination. If you have a taped declination arrow, you will have to peel the tape off and put a new one on, to correct for the new declination.

To take a bearing in the field, follow the same procedure used in the earlier examples for Mississippi. The only difference is that, from now on, you will align the magnetic needle with the declination arrow instead of with the orienting arrow. Always remember to align the north-seeking end of the magnetic needle with the pointed end of the declination arrow to box the needle.

From here on we will assume that you are using a compass with a declination arrow—either an adjustable arrow or a taped arrow that you have added. For all bearings in the field, you will align the needle with this declination arrow. All compass bearings used from this point on are true bearings. We will not refer to magnetic bearings again, since we always automatically convert all bearings to true ones using one of the two techniques described above.

BACK BEARINGS

A *back bearing* is the opposite direction of any given bearing. This is also sometimes referred to as a *reciprocal* bearing. Back bearings are often useful when you are trying to follow a certain bearing, and you want to check to see if you are still on the bearing line by taking a back bearing on your starting point. If your bearing is less than 180°, then you can find the back bearing by adding 180° to the original bearing. If your bearing is greater than 180°, then you can find the back bearing by subtracting 180° from the original bearing. For example, if you are traveling at a bearing of 90°, then the back bearing is 270°. Once you reach your destination, following the back bearing of 270° should get you back to your starting point.

We previously mentioned that we do not recommend mental arithmetic in the wilderness, since it is too easy to make mistakes. There are two other ways of dealing with back bearings, without using mental arithmetic. One way is to set your bearing at the index line of your compass, and then to look at the point on the compass dial opposite the index line. The number on the dial at this point is the back bearing (fig. 13). To follow this back bearing, set this number at the index line.

Another way of working with a back bearing is to set the original bearing at the index line, and position the direction-of-travel line to point at the back bearing by aligning the south-seeking end (the white or black end) of the magnetic needle with the pointed end of the declination arrow. The use of back bearings in wilderness navigation will be described in more detail in chapter 4.

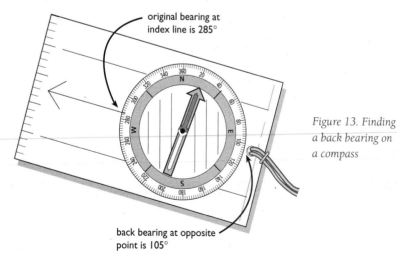

original bearing at
index line is 285°

back bearing at opposite
point is 105°

Figure 13. Finding a back bearing on a compass

BEARINGS ON THE MAP

You can use your compass as a protractor, both to measure and to plot bearings on a map. Magnetic north and magnetic declination have nothing to do with these operations. Therefore, ignore the magnetic needle when measuring or plotting bearings on a map. (The only time you need to use the magnetic needle when working with the map is whenever you choose to orient the map to true north, explained in chapter 3. But there is no need to orient the map to measure or plot bearings.)

To measure a bearing on a map: Place the compass on the map with one long edge of the base plate running between the two points of interest. To measure the bearing from point A to point B, make sure that the direction-of-travel line is pointing parallel to the direction from A to B (not the reverse). Then turn the rotating housing until its set of meridian lines is parallel to the north-south lines of the map. Be sure that the N on the compass dial is toward the top of the map and that the S is toward the bottom. (If you put the N toward the bottom of the map, with the S toward the top, your reading will be 180° off.) For the utmost in accuracy, slide the compass along the bearing line so that one of its meridian lines is exactly on top of one of the north-south lines on the map. Now read the number that is at the index line. This is the bearing from point A to point B.

Suppose you are at the summit of Panic Peak, and you want to know which of the many peaks around you is Deception Dome. Your map shows both peaks (fig. 14), so you can measure the bearing from point A, Panic Peak, to point B, Deception Dome. The result, as read at the index line, is 34°. (In this figure, we have purposely omitted the magnetic needle for the sake of clarity.) You can then hold the compass out in front of you and turn your entire body until you box the needle. The direction-of-travel line will then point toward Deception Dome and you can identify it.

Problems 17 and 24 in the appendix provide practice in measuring bearings from a map.

To plot a bearing on the map: In this case you are starting with a known bearing. And where does that bearing come from? From an actual landscape compass reading. Let us take a hypothetical example: Your friend returns from a backpacking trip, remorseful for having left a camera somewhere along the trail. While at a rest stop, your friend had taken a bearing on Mount Magnificent and found it to be 130°. That is all you need to know. You are heading into that same area next weekend, so get out the Mount Magnificent quadrangle, and here is what you do:

First set the bearing of 130° at the compass index line. Place the compass on the map, one long edge of the base plate touching the summit of Mount Magnificent (fig. 15). Rotate the entire compass (not

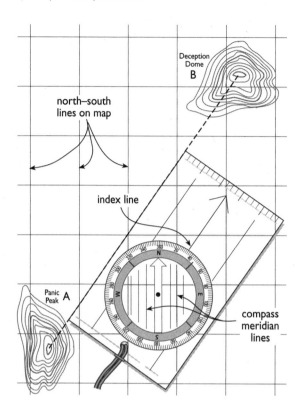

north–south lines on map

index line

compass meridian lines

Panic Peak A

Deception Dome B

Figure 14. Measuring a bearing on a map with the compass as a protractor (magnetic needle omitted for clarity)

just the housing) until the meridian lines in the compass housing are parallel with the map's north-south lines, and make sure that the edge of the base plate is still touching the summit. Again, make sure that the N on the compass dial is toward the top of the map. Draw a line along the edge of the base plate. Where this line crosses the trail is where your friend's camera is (or was).

Problems 18, 20, and 25 in the appendix involve plotting bearings on a map.

When measuring or plotting bearings on a map, the map does not need to be in a horizontal position, such as lying down on the snow or dirt, on a stump, or in the mud. Instead, it can be vertical or in any other position. Its orientation doesn't matter, since you are just using the compass as a protractor. In the forest, you can place the compass up against a tree to do the map and compass work. On a snowfield or glacier, with no trees, you can instead ask another member of the party to stand still while you steady the map against the person's back. Or you can sit down on your pack, and do the map work in your lap or on your knee with your leg crossed.

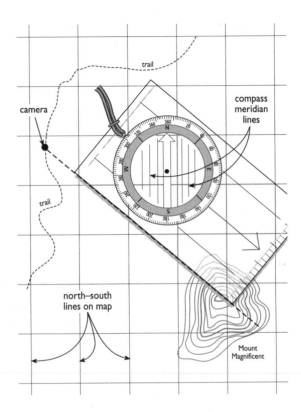

trail

camera

compass
meridian
lines

trail

*Figure 15.
Plotting a
bearing on a
map with the
compass as a
protractor
(magnetic
needle omitted
for clarity)*

north–south
lines on map

Mount
Magnificent

PRACTICING WITH THE COMPASS

Before you count on your compass skills in the wilderness, test them in an area near your home. The best place to practice is a place where you already know all the answers, such as at a street intersection where the roads run north-south and east-west.

Take a bearing in a direction you know to be east. When you have pointed the direction-of-travel line at something that you know is east of you, such as along the edge of the street or sidewalk, and have boxed the needle, the number at the index line should be very close to 90°. Repeat for the other cardinal directions: south, west, and north (see fig. 6). Then try all four again to see how repeatable the bearings are. Try to refine your technique to improve your accuracy. You may have to hold the compass higher or lower, or perhaps close one eye. Find out how accurate you can be. After some practice, you should consistently be able to get to within 2° of the correct bearing. This is usually adequate. If you cannot achieve this level of accuracy, or if you need better accuracy, you can get an optical sighting compass (see chapter 7).

Then try the reverse process. Pretend you do not know which way is west. Set 270° (west) at the index line and hold the compass out in front of you as you turn your entire body (including your feet) until the needle is boxed. The direction-of-travel line should now point west. Does it? Repeat for the other three cardinal directions (fig. 6). This set of exercises will help you to develop skill and self-confidence at compass reading and is also a way to check the accuracy of your compass. And if you make a mistake or two, well, no harm done.

You can practice measuring and plotting bearings on a map using the examples shown in figures 14 and 15. These figures are drawn with the correct angular proportions, so if you place your compass on the page you should get the same answers we get.

If you ever doubt the accuracy of your compass—perhaps because it has developed a small bubble or has given you a questionable reading in the field—take it out to the street intersection again to test it. If the bearings you read are more than a few degrees away from the correct ones, consider replacing your compass.

Look for places to practice in the wilderness. A good place is any known location (such as a summit or a lakeshore) from which you can see identifiable landmarks. Take bearings on some of these and plot them on the map to see how close the result is to your actual location.

TIPS ON COMPASS USE

There is a big difference between using a compass for working with a map and using a compass for fieldwork. In the field, you must box the needle by aligning the pointed end of the declination arrow with the red end of the magnetic needle. When measuring and plotting bearings on a map, however, you should ignore the compass needle. Just align the meridian lines in the compass housing with the north-south lines on the map, with the N of the compass dial toward north on the map. In both cases, the direction-of-travel line must point from you to your objective.

You may have heard that nearby metal can mess up a compass bearing. This is true. Ferrous objects such as iron and steel will deflect the magnetic needle and give false readings. Keep the compass away from belt buckles, ice axes, and other metal objects. Some wristwatches, particularly electronic ones, can also cause false readings if they are within a few inches of the compass. If a compass reading does not make sense, see if nearby metal is sabotaging your bearing.

Keep your wits about you when pointing the direction-of-travel line and the declination arrow. If you point either of them backward—an easy thing to do—the reading will be 180° off. If the bearing is north, the compass will say it is south. Remember that the north-seeking end of the magnetic needle must be aligned with the pointed end of the declination arrow and that the direction-of-travel line must point from you to your objective.

Whenever you measure or plot bearings on a map, it is a good idea to first guess at the answer, based on your knowledge of the cardinal directions (fig. 6). Then if the bearing you carefully measure or plot is nowhere near your original guess, you may have made one of those 180-degree errors. For example, suppose you want to measure a bearing on a map, and this bearing is somewhere between northeast (45°) and east (90°). You might guess that it is 60° to 80° or so. Then you measure the bearing as accurately as possible using your compass. You line up one of the compass meridian lines exactly on top of one of the map's north-south lines, getting the bearing accurate to the nearest degree, and the number you read at your index line is 247°. Does this agree with your original guess? No! You must have made a 180-degree mistake, and the correct answer is 67°.

When taking and following bearings in the field, you can also begin by making an intelligent guess at the result, then using the compass to get the exact answer. Before blindly following the compass, you can then ask yourself if the result from the compass agrees with your rough guess and common sense.

If in doubt, trust your compass. The compass, correctly used, is almost always right, while your contrary judgment may be clouded by fatigue, confusion, or hurry. If you get a nonsensical reading, check to see if perhaps you are making a 180-degree error. If not, and if no metal is nearby, verify the reading with other members of the party, using different compasses. If they get the same answer, trust your compass over hunches, blind guesses, and intuition.

THE MAP AND COMPASS: A CHECKLIST

Do you have the hang of it? There are four essential compass operations that you must learn: taking and following bearings in the field and measuring and plotting bearings on the map. Let us summarize these one last time. Check off each operation as you do it.

TO TAKE A BEARING IN THE FIELD

1. Hold compass level, in front of you, and point direction-of-travel line at desired object.
2. Rotate compass housing to align pointed end of declination arrow with red end of magnetic needle (box the needle).
3. Read bearing at index line.

TO FOLLOW A BEARING IN THE FIELD

1. Set desired bearing at index line.
2. Hold compass level, in front of you, and turn your entire body, including your feet, until red end of magnetic needle is aligned with pointed end of declination arrow (box the needle).
3. Travel in the direction shown by the direction-of-travel line.

TO MEASURE A BEARING ON A MAP (see fig. 14)

1. Place compass on map with one long edge of base plate joining two points of interest. Direction-of-travel line points to objective.
2. Rotate housing to align compass meridian lines with north-south lines on map, with N on compass towards top of map.
3. Read bearing at index line.

TO PLOT A BEARING ON A MAP (see fig. 15)

1. Set desired bearing at index line.
2. Place compass on map with one long edge of base plate on feature from which you wish to plot bearing.
3. Turn entire compass to align its meridian lines with map's north-south lines, with N on compass toward top of map. The edge of the base plate is now the bearing line.

Whenever you perform any of these operations, first guess at the answer, and perform the operation as accurately as you can. Then compare your answer to your original guess to ensure that you are not making a 180-degree error.

AND FOR THE LAST TIME:

▶ When taking and following bearings in the field, always align the pointed end of the declination arrow with the north-seeking end of the magnetic needle (box the needle).

▶ Never use the magnetic needle or the declination arrow when measuring or plotting bearings on the map. Just make sure that the N on the compass dial is toward north on the map, not south, as a check to ensure that the compass meridian lines are not upside-down.

Once you master these four essential operations with the compass, you will have all the knowledge you need for map-and-compass orientation, navigation, and routefinding. The remainder of this book is based on these operations. If you thoroughly understand how to do them, you can proceed through the rest of the book with confidence, and you will easily understand everything that we explain.

If you are unsure of any of these four operations, we suggest that you stop now and reread this chapter. Study it carefully. Do the simple street-corner compass exercises we described for taking and following bearings. Measure and plot the bearings shown in figures 14 and 15. Additional practice problems are given in the appendix. You must thoroughly understand each of these operations before proceeding with the rest of this book.

See chapter 7 for additional information on compasses and geomagnetism. You are particularly urged to read chapter 7 if you ever plan to travel to foreign lands on distant continents, where you may not know the declination, or where the compass may be adversely affected by magnetic dip.

Once you thoroughly understand the basics, you are ready for orientation with map and compass.

Orientation with Map and Compass

Figuring out your exact location is usually relatively simple. Just look around and compare what you see with what is on a map. Sometimes this is not accurate enough, or there is just nothing much nearby to identify on the map. The usual solution then is to get out the compass and to try for bearings on some landscape features. This is orientation by instrument. But before resorting to orientation by instrument, first study the map carefully to see if there are any topographic features—even subtle ones—that you can associate with the landscape around you. If you have been carefully observing your map and comparing it with the landscape, as we suggested in chapter 1, you should have a fairly good idea of where you are. Orientation by instrument should be reserved for those situations in which nothing else works, for compass practice, or for verifying your location after using other methods.

The goal of orientation is to determine that precise point on the surface of the earth where you now stand. You can represent your position by a mere dot on the map. This is known as *point position*. There are two lower levels of orientation. One is called *line position:* you know you are along a certain line on a map—such as a river, a trail, a ridge, a compass bearing, or a contour line—but you do not where you are along the line. The lowest level of orientation is *area position:* you know the general area you are in, but that is all. The objective of orientation is to determine your exact point position.

POINT POSITION

With point position known, you know exactly where you are, and you can use that knowledge to identify on the map any major feature that you can see in the landscape. You can also identify in the landscape any major visible feature that is shown on the map.

For example, suppose you have hiked to the summit of Blue Mountain (fig. 16). You know your point position: the top of Blue Mountain. You see an unknown peak and want to know what it is. You take a compass bearing on it and get 232°. You plot 232° from Blue Mountain on your map, and the plotted line passes through Green Mountain. The unknown peak is Green Mountain.

However, if you start by wanting to determine which of the many peaks around you is Green Mountain, you must do the map work first. You measure the bearing on the map from where you are, Blue Mountain, to Green Mountain and get 232°. Keeping the 232° at the index line, turn the entire compass until the needle is boxed. The direction-of-travel line then points toward Green Mountain.

LINE POSITION

With line position known, the goal is to determine point position. If you know that you are on a trail, ridge, or some other easily identifiable line, you need only one more trustworthy piece of information to get your point position. For example, suppose a party of scramblers is

Figure 16. Example of point position

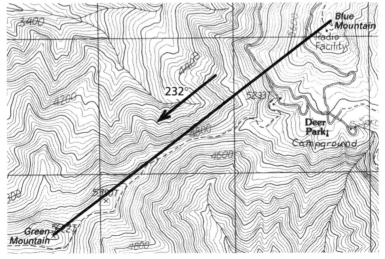

on Unsavory Ridge (fig. 17), but they do not know exactly where they are on the ridge. In the distance is Mount Majestic. A bearing on it indicates 220°. They plot 220° from Mount Majestic on the map, and run this line back toward Unsavory Ridge. Where it intersects the ridge is where the scramblers are.

AREA POSITION

Some snowshoers know their area position: they are in the general area of Fantastic Crags. They want to determine line position and then, from that, point position. To move from knowing area position to knowing point position, they need two trustworthy pieces of information (fig. 18).

They may be able to use bearings on two visible features. They take a bearing on Fantastic Peak and get a reading of 40°. They plot a line on the map, along the base plate and through Fantastic Peak, at 40°. They know they must be somewhere on that bearing line, so they now have line position. They can also see Unsavory Spire. A bearing on the spire shows 130°. They plot this line on the map, through Unsavory Spire, and draw a line along the base plate. The two bearing lines intersect, and that is their location.

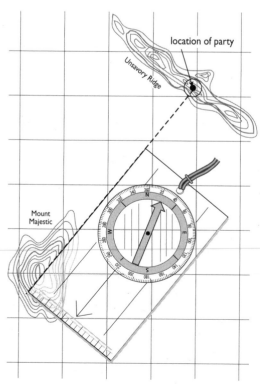

Figure 17. Orientation with line position known (magnetic needle omitted for clarity)

Or approximately so. Whenever you take a bearing in the field or plot a bearing on a map, it is inevitable that minor errors will creep in to create larger errors in the estimate of your position. It is very easy to make an error of 3° in taking a bearing and another 2° in plotting that bearing unless you are extremely careful. For every 5° of error, your position will be in error by about 460 feet in every mile (about 90 meters in every kilometer). If you take and plot a bearing on a landmark 3 miles away and make a 5-degree error, the plotted line might be about 1400 feet away from the correct position. Therefore, be sure that your conclusions agree with common sense. If you take and plot bearings from two peaks and find that the two lines intersect in the middle of a river, but you are standing on a high point of land, something is wrong. Try again. Try to take a more accurate bearing and plot it more carefully. If bearing lines intersect at a map location with no similarity to the terrain, you may have errors in your bearings, or there

Figure 18. Orientation with area position known (magnetic needle omitted for clarity)

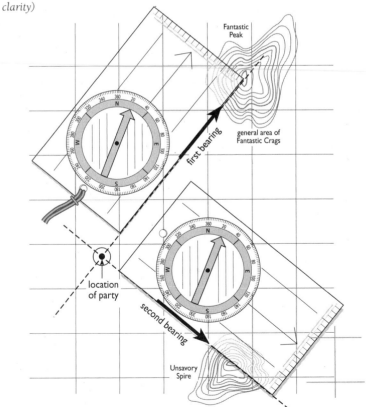

might be some magnetic anomaly in the rocks, or you might have an inaccurate map. And who knows? Maybe those peaks are not really the peaks you think they are. Make sure that the two bearings are not from approximately the same direction, since this can compound any error. The closer an angle of intersection is to 90°, the more accurate the point position will be.

The technique of taking and plotting bearings from landmarks is more accurate if you can see *three* landmarks and plot three bearings. The result will be a small triangle called a "cocked hat" (see fig. 19). Your position is most likely within this triangle.

Problems 19, 23, 26, and 28 in the appendix provide practice in orientation by plotting bearings on a map.

ORIENTING A MAP

During a trip it sometimes helps to hold the map so that north on the map is pointed in the actual direction of true north. This is known as orienting the map, a good way to obtain a better feel of the relationship between the map and the countryside.

One way to orient a map is *by inspection:* simply look at the terrain and compare it to the map. Then hold the map level and turn it until the map is lined up with the terrain.

Often, this technique will not work because you cannot see any identifiable features around you. In this case, you can orient your map using your compass. Set 360° (north) at the index line of the compass and place your compass on the map. Put one long edge of the base plate along the left edge of the map as shown in figure 20, with

Figure 19. Plotting three bearings results in a "cocked hat" position.

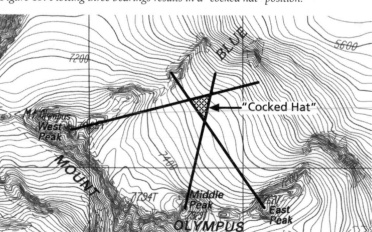

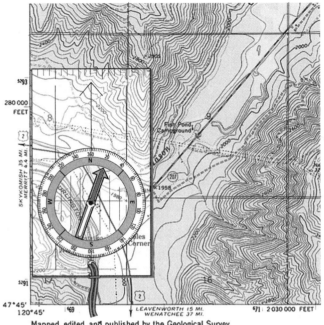

Figure 20. Using the compass to orient a map in an area with 20 degrees east declination

the N of the compass dial pointing to the direction of north on the map. Then turn the map and compass together until the needle is boxed. The map is now oriented to the scene around you. (Map orientation can give you a general feel for the area but cannot replace the precise methods of orientation that we covered in the preceding paragraphs.)

DIRECTION AND BEARING OF THE SLOPE

You can often help to find your position by using the *direction of the slope,* which was first described in chapter 1. For example, suppose you are hiking along the trail near Maiden Peak (fig. 21) and want to find your point position. You take a bearing on Maiden Peak and get 242°. You plot this bearing and find that it crosses the trail in two places, A and B. Where are you? Points A and B are both on a ridge, but at point A the slope falls off to the east, while at point B it falls off to the north. Suppose you take your compass and point it in the direction of the slope. You find that the actual slope falls off to the north. That tells you that you are at point B, not point A.

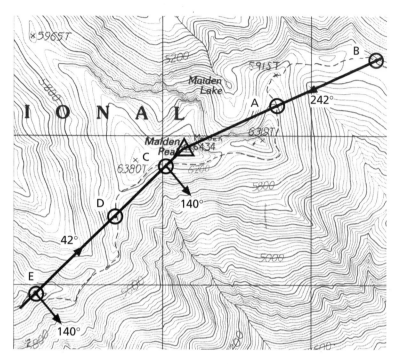

Figure 21. Using the bearing of the slope to find your position

Sometimes the situation is a little more subtle, so we need more accuracy with this approach. In this case, we refer to the *bearing of the slope* rather than merely its general direction. Imagine that another party is also on the Maiden Peak trail and wants to find its position. Some party members take a bearing on Maiden Peak and get 42°. They plot this line, as shown in figure 21, and they see that the bearing line crosses the trail in *three* places. Where are they, point C, D, or E? A quick compass bearing shows that the slope falls off roughly to the southeast, so point D is ruled out, since at that point the map clearly shows the slope to fall off to the east. That narrows it down to either point C or point E. A party member faces downhill and takes a more careful bearing in the direction of the fall line. Suppose the bearing is 140°. One long edge of the compass is then placed on the map at point C, and the entire compass is rotated until the meridian lines in the compass housing are parallel with the north-south lines on the map, with the N on the compass dial toward the top of the map. The edge of the base plate should then point in a direction perpendicular to the contour lines at point C. However, you can see that the bearing of 140° is *not* perpendicular to the contour lines at point C. So instead, the same process can be repeated for point E. This time, the bearing line is nearly perpendicular to the contour lines, at least for the first 200 feet down from point E. From this, the party concludes that it is at point E.

Problems 8 and 16 in the appendix involve measuring the direction of the slope on a map.

A REMINDER

At the beginning of this chapter we said that orientation by instrument should be reserved for those situations in which nothing else works. The best method of orientation is to use your map and your continual observations of topography to keep track of where you are. Presumably at the beginning of your trek, you know where you are and can identify that position on the map. If you then follow your progress on the map, noting each topographic or other feature that you pass, then at any time you should know your position with a great amount of certainty. It is essential to know the technical methods of map and compass orientation, but there is still no substitute for keeping track of your position using the map.

Once you have mastered the science of orientation and can determine exactly where you are, you are ready for navigation using map and compass.

Navigation with Map and Compass

Getting from here to there is usually just a matter of keeping an eye on the landscape and watching where you are going, helped by an occasional glance at the map. However, if you cannot see your objective in the field, you can measure the bearing on the map, then take compass in hand and follow the direction-of-travel line as it guides you to the goal. This is navigation by instrument. It is a technique that will work if you are able to follow a straight-line route, something often impossible in wilderness terrain. For this reason, it is best to first try to follow topographic features in off-trail wilderness navigation and to reserve navigation by instrument for situations where the topography lacks sufficient features to be of any help to you.

Navigation by instrument is sometimes the only practical method for finding a crucial pass, base camp, or other goal. It also serves as a supplement to other methods, such as following topographic features, and it can help to verify that you are on the right track. Again use common sense and challenge a compass reading that defies reason. (Is your declination arrow or direction-of-travel line pointing the wrong way, sending you 180° off course?)

MAP AND COMPASS

The most common situation requiring instrument navigation comes when the route is unclear because the topography is featureless or because landmarks are obscured by forest or fog. You know exactly where you are and exactly where you want to go, and you can identify both your present position and your destination on the map. In this case, simply measure the bearing from your present position to your objective on the map, and then follow that bearing to your objective. Suppose you measure a bearing of 285° on the map (fig. 22a). Read this bearing at the index line and leave it set there (fig. 22b). Then hold your compass out in front of you as you rotate your body until you have boxed the needle. The direction-of-travel line now points to your objective (fig. 22c). Start walking.

Figure 22. Navigation using the map and compass (on a and b, magnetic needle omitted for clarity): a. measuring the bearing on the map from your position to your destination, b. reading the bearing at the index line (leave the compass set), c. following the bearing

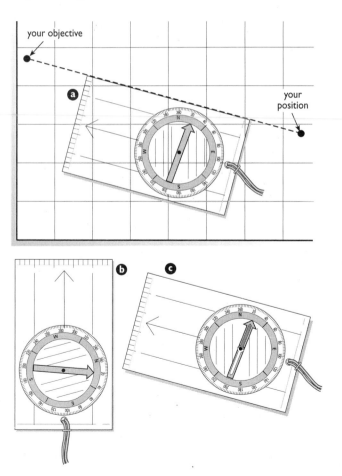

COMPASS ALONE

Navigators of air and ocean often travel by instrument alone; you can too. For example, suppose you are scrambling toward a pass and clouds begin to obscure your view. Just take a quick compass bearing on the pass before it disappears from view. Then follow that bearing, compass in hand if you wish. You do not even have to note the numerical bearing; just box the needle and keep it boxed as you proceed to your objective. Likewise, if you are heading into a valley where fog or forest will hide your goal, take a bearing on the goal before you drop into the valley, and then follow that bearing after you lose sight of the objective (fig. 23). This method becomes more reliable if several people travel together, checking each other's work by taking occasional back bearings on each other.

Figure 23. Following a compass bearing when the view of the objective is obscured by forest or fog

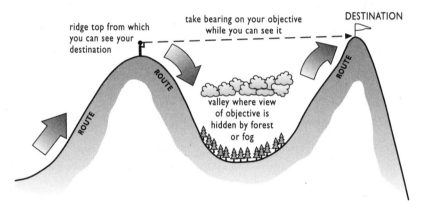

USING INTERMEDIATE OBJECTIVES

A handy technique is available for those frustrating times when you try to travel exactly along a compass bearing but are frequently diverted by obstructions such as cliffs, dense brush, or crevasses. Try the technique of intermediate objectives. If in a forest, sight past the obstruction to a tree or rock or other object that is exactly on the bearing line to the principal objective (fig. 24a). Then you are free to travel over to the tree or rock by whatever route is easiest. When you get to the intermediate objective, you can be confident that you are still on the correct route. This technique is useful even when there is no obstruction. Moving from one intermediate objective to another means you can put the compass away for those stretches, rather than having to hold it continually in your hand and check it every few steps.

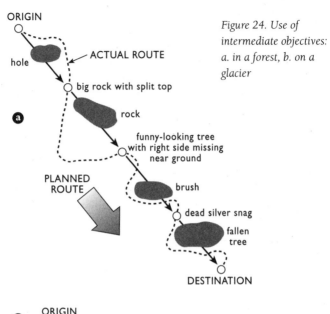

Figure 24. Use of intermediate objectives: a. in a forest, b. on a glacier

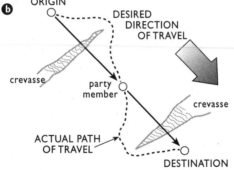

Sometimes on snow or glaciers, in fog, or in a forest where all the trees look the same, there are no natural intermediate objectives. In this case, another member of the party can serve as the target (fig. 24b). Send some party members out to near the limit of visibility or past the obstruction. Wave them left or right until they are directly on the bearing line. They can improve the accuracy of the route by taking a back bearing on you.

THE INTENTIONAL OFFSET ("AIMING OFF")

Now imagine that your party is almost back to the car after a scramble. You follow a compass bearing to the logging road, but you cannot see the car because you are off route by a few degrees. You have to guess which way to go. It is a bad ending to the trip if the car is to the right

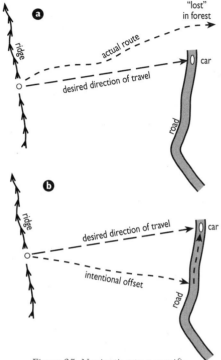

Figure 25. *Navigating to a specific point on a line: a. inevitable minor errors can sometimes have disastrous consequences, b. to avoid such problems, follow a course with an intentional offset*

and you go left. It will be even worse if the car is parked at the end of the road, and a route-finding error takes the party beyond that point and on and on through the woods (fig. 25a). The *intentional offset* (also called "aiming off") was invented for this situation (fig. 25b). Just travel in a direction that is intentionally offset by 20° to 30° to the right or the left of wherever you want to be. When you hit the road, there will be no doubt about which way to turn.

THE PARALLEL PATH

One of the most vexing navigational problems can be the situation encountered when traveling in a direction that parallels the direction of a road, trail, or other feature to which you must return in order to get back home. Such a situation is illustrated in figure 26. A party drives along a fairly straight road to its end, parks the car, and hikes to the objective in a direction exactly parallel to the road. Both the road and the objective are clearly visible on the map, so once at the objective, the party can measure the bearing back to the road end. When following this bearing back, however, it is impossible to stay exactly on route, due to irregularities in the topography. Consequently, when the party nears the car, it may have missed the end of the road and ended up in the woods to either the right or the left of the road. With a little forethought, they could have avoided this situation by using a variation of the aiming off technique. They could have purposely taken a route 20° to 30° to the right of the correct path, to a point safely past the end of the road. Once sure they were past this point, they could then turn sharply left, and they would soon intersect the road. A short hike up the road would then lead them back to the car. The overall trip would be longer than if they had taken a direct path, but the latter might have caused them to miss the road entirely.

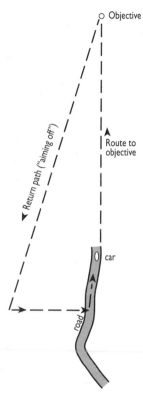

Figure 26. Example of traveling on a path parallel to a road, trail, or other line position

NAVIGATING AROUND AN OBSTRUCTION

Sometimes you try to follow a constant bearing to get to your objective, but find that the route is blocked by an obstruction such as a lake or a cliff. There may be an easy way to get around the obstruction, but doing so forces you off your intended bearing. What do you do?

If the obstruction is a lake or swamp, you may be able to see across it back to your starting point after you have traveled past it (fig. 27). In this case, try to find some large, easily visible object on your bearing line before you start traveling past the obstruction. If that point is a nondescript location with no identifiable landmark, you can mark this spot with a streamer of toilet paper or other material which will rapidly deteriorate in the next storm. Once you know that you have an identifiable object or marker along your bearing line, you can walk around the obstruction using whatever route is easiest. Once past the obstruction, take a back bearing on your starting point. If this does not match the bearing of your intended direction-of-travel, then continue around the obstruction until your back bearing on the starting point does match your intended direction-of-travel.

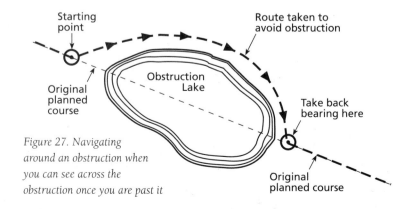

Figure 27. Navigating around an obstruction when you can see across the obstruction once you are past it

If the obstruction is a cliff, a hill, or some other feature that prevents you from seeing your starting point once you have passed the obstruction, then you may have to use a different technique as shown in figure 28. In this case, you can travel a paced distance at 90° to the original course, then go past the blockage on a bearing parallel to the original course, and finally return to the original course by another 90-degree course change paced the same distance as the earlier one but in the opposite direction. (The course change need not be 90°. It could be 45° or some other direction, as long as it is easily possible to return to the original direction-of-travel.)

ALWAYS KNOW WHERE YOU ARE HEADED, AND CONSIDER THE RETURN ROUTE

No party should ever wander off on what may appear to be an obvious route without knowing the direction they are heading and considering how they will return. Consider the example of a party that follows a trail to a camp in the forest (fig. 29). After setting up camp and eating dinner, they decide to hike off-trail to a clearly visible pass to see the view. After enjoying a memorable sunset at the pass, they turn around to return to camp. At that point it occurs to them that they cannot see their camp, do not know the direction to it, and will shortly be running out of daylight. Is this a problem? It all depends on the preparations they made on the trip to the pass. If they merely headed up to the pass without any thought of how they would get back, they might be in trouble. If, on the other hand, they had taken a compass bearing

Figure 28. Navigating around an obstruction when the view across the obstruction is blocked

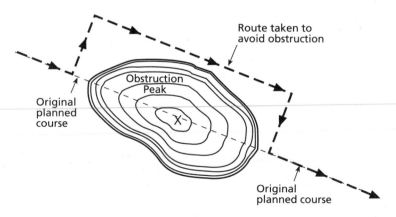

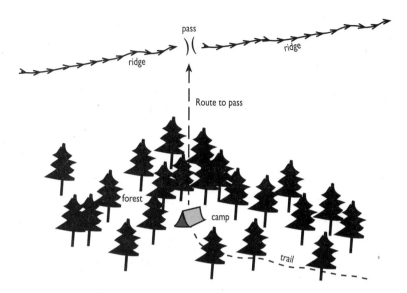

Figure 29. Example of traveling via obvious route to a destination from which the return trip will not be obvious

from their camp to the pass when they started their trek, then once at the pass, they could simply follow a back bearing from the pass to return to their camp in the forest. They could also use route-marking materials, such as a streamer of toilet paper, to mark the spot where they emerged from the forest. These simple measures could turn a potentially serious problem into a routine after-dinner stroll.

A REMINDER

At the start of this chapter we recommended using topographic features whenever possible in off-trail navigation and using navigation by instrument only for those situations in which the topography lacks sufficient features. Now, after describing eight different techniques used in off-trail navigation, we are concerned that you might have forgotten the original point, so we will repeat it: wherever possible, navigate by using natural topographic features. Reserve the use of navigation by instrument for those situations where there is no alternative.

If you have thoroughly mastered the sciences of orientation and navigation, and if you keep these principles in mind as you navigate toward your objective and back, it is unlikely that you will ever get lost.

Chapter 5

Lost!

> **Note:** If you turned to this chapter first, after seeing its title in the table of contents, please **go back** to the beginning of the book and read chapters 1 through 4 before reading this chapter. The focus of this chapter is to prevent you from getting lost, which requires a thorough knowledge of map, compass, orientation, and navigation.

The primary focus of this book is to give you the necessary skills and knowledge to avoid getting lost in the first place. Later in this chapter we will give you some suggestions concerning what to do if you ever *do* get lost. But if you have carefully read and absorbed the preceding four chapters, carry a compass and a topographic map of the area, and have adequately practiced map reading, compass use, orientation, and navigation, you should always know where you are. If so, you are not lost, and this entire subject may be only of academic interest to you. In addition to the information provided in the first four chapters, the information given in this chapter may go a long way toward preventing you from ever getting lost.

HOW TO AVOID GETTING LOST
Before the Trip

Most wilderness orientation, navigation, and routefinding is done by simply looking at your surroundings and comparing them to the map. This process is often aided by making some navigational preparations before the trip, such as identifying *handrails*, *baselines*, and possible routefinding problems.

A handrail is a linear feature on the map that you can follow, or it may be a feature that parallels the direction in which you are heading. The handrail should be within frequent sight of the route, so it can serve as an aid in navigation. Features that you can use from time to time as handrails during a trip include roads, trails, powerlines, railroad tracks, fences, borders of fields and meadows, valleys, streams, cliff bands, ridges, lakeshores, and the edges of marshes.

A baseline is a long, unmistakable line that always lies in the same direction from you, no matter where you are during the trip. Pick out a baseline on the map during trip planning. It does not have to be something you can see during the trip. You just have to know that it is there, in a consistent direction from you. A baseline (sometimes called a *catch line*) can be a road, an obvious trail, the shore of a large lake, a river, a powerline, or any other feature that is at least as long as your trip area. If the shore of a distant lake always lies west of the area you will be in, you can be sure that heading west at any time will eventually get you to this identifiable landmark. Heading toward this baseline may not be the fastest way to travel back home from your destination, but it may save you from being truly lost.

For example, a party once began a long scramble but was turned around due to bad weather. They started to drive home but had a flat tire on the way. While two people changed the tire, the others noticed some delicious edible mushrooms alongside the road. A little exploration revealed that the deeper into the woods they ventured, the more numerous and luscious the mushrooms became. They told the others, and after the tire was changed they all decided to dump their pack contents in the trunk of the car and head out into the woods to fill their packs with mushrooms. After an hour or so all the packs were filled with mushrooms, but the party had not noticed where they had been going, had taken no compass bearings, and had not followed any recognizable topographic features, since the terrain was flat and featureless. Was this a problem? Not really. They knew that the road they were traveling ran almost true north-south (fig. 30). They also knew that they had not crossed the road, so they must have been on the east side of the road. Some party members had their compasses in their pockets so they could easily set their compasses on a course due west. A short ramble in the woods brought them back to the road, and they could see their car. This is a classic example of baseline navigation.

Before the trip, it is wise to prepare a *route plan* and to trace out the entire trip on a topographic map. Identify handrails, baselines, and other features that you will be following on the way to your objective. Part of this plan is to recognize potential routefinding problems. For

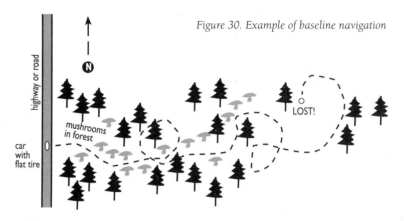

Figure 30. Example of baseline navigation

example, if the route traverses a large, featureless area, you may need route-marking materials, particularly if the weather outlook is marginal. Be sure to carry such materials if your route plan indicates a possible need for them. Make a note of any escape routes that can be used in case of sudden bad weather or other setbacks. If off-trail travel is involved, measure compass bearings at home before the trip and write them down in a notebook or note them on the map. It is certainly possible to measure map bearings at any point in the trip, but it is easier at home on your kitchen table and might save you time in an emergency. Write down and discuss your route plan with other members of the party, so the party is not solely dependent on one person for all route decisions. You might consider requiring all party members (or at least children or inexperienced persons) to carry whistles.

Another thing you should do before the trip is to tell a responsible person where you are going, what route you are taking, and when you plan on returning. This will not prevent you from getting lost. But if you *do* run into trouble, the authorities will know to look for you—and where to look. This one bit of preparation could save your life.

Always make sure that every member of the party carries adequate food, clothing, and other supplies (see "Survival" below). In the event of an emergency, each person should have enough food and clothing to survive several days, if necessary, while waiting for search and rescue personnel to arrive. Every party member should carry a map of the area and a compass, in case someone becomes separated from the group.

During the Trip

Get off on the right foot by making sure that everyone understands the route and the route plan. Gather the party around a map and take time to discuss the route and to make contingency plans in case the party becomes separated. Point out on the map where you are, and associate your surroundings with the piece of paper in front of you. This is a good time for everyone to make a mental note of the main features—such as forests, streams, ridges, valleys, mountain peaks, and trails—that they will see during the trip.

Along the way, everyone needs to continue associating the terrain with the map. Ignorance of the territory is definitely not bliss for any day-dreaming person who becomes separated from the party. Whenever a new landmark appears, connect it with the map. At every chance—at a pass, in a clearing, or through a break in the clouds—update your fix on the group's exact position. Keeping track of your progress this way makes it easy to plan each succeeding leg of the trip. It may also turn you into an expert map reader because you will quickly learn what a specific valley or ridge looks like compared to its representation on the map.

Use handrails wherever possible. When the inevitable moment comes for you to leave the security of your handrail, make a mental note of the fact that you are leaving it, and ask yourself what you will be following instead—some topographic feature, a contour line, a compass bearing, or anything else you can count on. You should not merely press onward without a clear idea of where you are headed, or how to get back.

Keep the party together, except perhaps on well-traveled, obvious trails. Even then do not let the group get too spread out, and agree ahead of time on places to stop and wait for everyone to catch up. If the group includes children or inexperienced persons, keep them in sight at all times. Assign a responsible, experienced person to be the rear guard, or "sweep," to ensure that no straggler will be left behind or lost.

Look Ahead to the Return Trip

The route always looks amazingly different on the way back to the trailhead. Avoid surprises and confusion by glancing over your shoulder often on the way in to see what the route should look like on the return. If you cannot keep track of it all, jot down times, elevations, landmarks, and so on in a small notebook. A few cryptic words, such as "7600, hit ridge," can save you a lot of grief on the return. It will remind you that when the party has dropped to 7600 feet, it is time to leave the ridge and start down the slope to your starting point.

Think

Your brain is your most important navigational tool, a fact often overlooked amid our reliance on compasses, altimeters, GPS receivers, and other gadgets. As the party heads toward its destination, keep asking yourself questions: How will we recognize this important spot on our return? What would we do if the trip leader became unconscious? (Are we all placing total reliance on one person?) Could I find my way back if I had to? Would we be able to find our way back in a whiteout, or if snow covered our tracks? Should we be marking the route right now? Ask the questions as you go, and act on your answers. It may be a matter of think now or pay later.

Mark the Route if Necessary

There are times when it may be best to mark the route going in so you can find it again on the way out. This situation can occur when the route passes over snowfields or glaciers during changeable weather, in heavy forest, or when fog threatens to hide landmarks. On snow, climbers use thin bamboo wands with little flags to mark the path (see "Wands" in chapter 10). In the forest, plastic surveyor's tape is sometimes tied to branches to show the route, but we discourage its use due to its permanence, since we always endeavor to leave no trace. From an ecological standpoint, toilet paper is the best marker, because it will disintegrate during the next rainfall. Use toilet paper only if you are assured of good weather. If not, use brightly colored crepe paper in thin rolls. It will survive the next storm, but it will most likely disintegrate during the winter.

One strong admonition here: *remove your markers.* Markers are litter, and good wilderness travelers never, ever litter. If there is any chance that you will not come back the same way and will not be able to remove the markers, be especially sure to use biodegradable markers.

Rock cairns appear here and there as markers, sometimes dotting an entire route and at other times signaling the point where a route changes direction. These heaps of rock are another imposition on the landscape, and they can create confusion for any traveler but the one who put them together—so do not build them. If there ever comes a time when you decide you must, then do so, but tear them down on the way out. The rule is different, however, for existing cairns. Leave them alone, on the assumption that someone else may be depending on them. Your goal should be to leave the landscape exactly as *you* found it.

Keep Track

As the trip goes on, it may be helpful to mark your progress on the map. Keep yourself oriented so that at any time you can point out your actual position to within half a mile (1 km) on the map.

Part of keeping track is having a sense of your speed. Given all the variables, will it take your party 1 hour to travel 2 miles, or will it take 2 hours to travel 1 mile? The answer is important if it is 3:00 P.M. and base camp is still 5 miles away. After enough trips into the wilds, you will be good at estimating travel speeds. Here are some typical speeds for an average party, though there will be much variation:

- On a gentle trail, with a day pack: 2 to 3 miles (3 to 5 km) per hour
- Up a steep trail, with a full overnight pack: 1 to 2 miles (1.5 to 3 km) per hour
- Traveling up a moderate slope, with a day pack: 1000 feet (about 300 m) of elevation gain per hour
- Traveling up a moderate slope, with a full overnight pack: 500 feet (about 150 m) of elevation gain per hour

In heavy brush, your rate of travel can drop to a third or even a quarter of what it would be on a good trail. Above 10,000 feet (about 3000 m), your rate of travel will also greatly decrease, perhaps to as little as a hundred feet (30 m) of elevation gain per hour, depending on your condition and your state of acclimatization. On the descent if the terrain is easy, such as on a good trail or a snowfield, your rate of progress can be twice the speed of the ascent, or even more.

With a watch and a notebook (or a really good memory), you can monitor your rate of progress on any outing. Always make sure to note your starting time as well as the times you reach important streams, ridges, trail junctions, and other points along the route.

Experienced wilderness travelers regularly assess their party's progress and compare it with the route plan. Estimate and reestimate when you will reach your destination and when you will return to your base camp or starting point. If it begins to look as though your party could become trapped in tricky terrain during darkness, you may decide to change your plans and bivouac in a safe place, or call it a day and return home.

At Your Destination

Here is your golden opportunity to rest, relax, and enjoy—and to learn more about the area and about map reading by comparing the actual view with the way it looks on the map. Your destination is also the place to lay final plans for the return, a journey often responsible for many more routefinding problems than the way in. Repeat the trailhead get-together by discussing the route plan and emergency strategies with everyone. Stress the importance of keeping the party together on the return. Invariably, some will want to race ahead while others lag behind.

During the Return Trip

The return trip is a time for extra caution as you fight fatigue and inattention. As on the trip in, everyone needs to maintain a good sense of the route and how it relates to the map. Stay together, do not rush, and be even more careful if you are taking a different return route.

After the Trip

Back home while the details are fresh in your mind, write a detailed description of the route and any problems, mistakes, or unusual features. Imagine what you would like to know if you were about to do the trip for the first time, so you will be ready with the right answers when another person asks about it. If a guidebook was confusing or wrong, take the time to write to the publisher.

WHAT IF YOU *DO* GET LOST?

Why do people get lost? For a lot of reasons. Some travel without a map because the route seems obvious. Others fail to check on recent changes in roads and trails. Some people trust their own instincts over the compass. Others do not bother with the map homework that can start them off with a good mental picture of the area. Some do not pay enough attention to the route on the way in, to be able to find it on the way out. Some rely on the skill of their partner, who is just then in the process of getting them lost. Others do not think about where they are going, because they are in a hurry. Some miss junctions or wander off on game trails. Still others charge mindlessly ahead despite deteriorating weather and visibility, fatigue, or flagging spirits.

Good wilderness travelers are never truly lost—but having learned humility through years of experience, they always carry enough food, clothing, and bivouac gear to get them through hours or even days of temporary confusion.

What If Your Party Is Lost?

The first rule is to *stop*. In fact, even if you *think* you might not be where you should be, *stop!* Resist the temptation to press onward. The moment you are ever unsure of your position, you should stop. Try to determine where you are. Keep your wits about you and do not forget what you have learned about map reading and using the compass. Study the shape of the terrain and try to associate it with the map to find out where you are. Remember the technique of the *bearing of the slope*. Take a bearing on the fall line and try to associate it with your position by studying the map. If these suggestions do not work, then try to figure out the last time the group *did* know its exact location. If that spot is fairly close, within an hour or so, retrace your steps and get back on route. But if that spot is hours back, you might instead decide to head toward the baseline. If it begins to look as though darkness will fall before you can get back, you might have to bivouac for the night. If so, start looking for an adequate place, with water and some sort of shelter if possible, well before dark.

Some hopelessly lost parties have been found by rescuers when they dialed 911 on their cell phones. If you have a cell phone, it might be a good idea to carry it into the wilderness, as an added precaution. You must be aware, however, that such phones do not always work in all terrain or in all locations. They must be able to transmit and receive signals to and from the nearest cell tower, which might be out of range for many areas in the wilderness. Battery life is limited, and the signals can sometimes be blocked by mountains or other topographic features. So even if you carry a cell phone, you should never consider it to be a completely dependable way of being found if you are lost. You should still take all necessary steps to avoid getting lost, as described earlier in this chapter.

Being lost in a party is bad enough, but it is even worse when an individual is alone and separated from the rest of the party. For this reason, always try to keep everyone together, and assign a rear guard to keep track of any stragglers. If you ever notice that someone is missing, the entire party should stop, stay together, shout, and listen for answering shouts.

What If You Are Lost Alone?

Again, the first rule is to *stop*. Look around for other members of the party, shout, and listen for answering shouts. Sound your whistle if you have one. If the only answer is silence, sit down, calm down, and combat terror with reason.

Once you have calmed down, start doing the right things. Look at your map in an attempt to determine your location, and plan a route home in case you do not connect with the rest of the party. Mark your location with a cairn or other objects, and then scout in all directions, each time returning to your marked position. Well before dark, prepare for the night by finding water, firewood, and shelter. Staying busy will raise your spirits. Keep a fire going to give searchers something to see, and try singing (no matter how bad a singer you are) so you will have something to do and they will have something to hear.

The odds are that you will be reunited with your group by morning. If not, fight panic. After a night alone, you may decide to hike out to a baseline feature—a ridge, stream, or highway—that you picked out before the trip. If the terrain is too difficult to travel alone, it might be better to concentrate on letting yourself be found. It is far easier for rescuers to find a lost person who stays in one place in the open, builds a fire, and shouts periodically, than one who thrashes on in hysterical hope, one step ahead of the rescue party.

The decision whether to forge ahead or to stay put is strongly influenced by whether or not anyone knows you are missing and where to look for you. If you are traveling alone, or if your entire party is lost, and no one knows you are missing, or where you had planned to go, you have no choice but to try to find your way back, even if this involves difficult travel. If, on the other hand, someone responsible expects you back at a certain time and knows where you were planning to go and what route you planned to take, then you have the option of staying put, making yourself visible, and concentrating on survival while waiting for a search party to find you.

Survival

Your chances for survival depend on how well equipped you are. Numerous stories of survival and tragedy start with statements such as, "I was sure glad I had my . . . ," or "Too bad they did not bring a . . ." Over the years these crucial items of gear have developed into a codified list known as The Ten Essentials: A Systems Approach.

1. Navigation system: This contains, as a minimum, a topographic map of the area and a compass. It might also include an altimeter, a GPS receiver, and route-marking materials.
2. Sun protection: Sunglasses and sunscreen.
3. Insulation: Enough extra clothing to survive the most severe night that you can expect in the area you will be visiting.
4. Illumination system: A flashlight or headlamp, plus spare batteries and a spare bulb.
5. First-aid supplies: Including any prescription medications that you take on a daily basis, in case you do not make it back home in time for the next dose.
6. Fire system: Matches in a waterproof case and firestarter.
7. Repair kit and tools: At a minimum, a good, multibladed knife. Add other tools depending on what equipment you might need to maintain.
8. Nutrition: In addition to snacks for the day, carry enough extra food to survive for at least an extra day.
9. Hydration system: Adequate water plus possibly some water purification method.
10. Emergency shelter: A plastic tube tent, for example.

Always consider the possibility that one member of your party might become separated from the rest of the group and will depend totally on his or her own equipment and skill for survival. Thus it is essential for each person to carry adequate food and equipment. It is equally important that each person in the party have the knowledge and skill to use all the necessary equipment (including the map and the compass), rather than always relying on the skills of another. If someone gets lost, having the proper equipment and skills may make the difference between tragedy and a graceful recovery from the experience.

More about Maps

In chapter 1 we introduced the subject of maps and described the interpretation of colors and contour lines on topographic maps. In this chapter we will provide information on several other features of maps, including distance measurement, pace, slope measurement, and the range, township, and section system of land survey.

DISTANCE MEASUREMENT ON THE MAP

You can easily measure distances on the map using the scales at the bottom of the map. To measure a straight-line distance, simply measure the length of the line joining the two points of interest using the inch or centimeter scale of your compass. Then transfer this distance to one of the scales at the bottom of the map and read off the number of feet, meters, kilometers, or miles. If the distance on the map is greater than the length of your compass scale, or if the route is not a straight line, then use the lanyard attached to your compass. (If your compass does not have a lanyard, you can easily create one by tying a spare shoelace to the compass through the slot made for the lanyard.) Put the free end of the lanyard on one point on the map, then place the lanyard on the route to be measured, curving it along the trail, ridge, or other feature, until it reaches the other point on the map. Then straighten out the lanyard and place it alongside the desired scale at the bottom of the map. While following trails with numerous short switchbacks, this method may be inaccurate, since the lanyard may not be able to keep up with all the tiny zigzags. In this case, your map measurement will at least give you a minimum distance, which may be enough information. (Map measuring instruments are also available, but these are generally no more accurate than the lanyard method and add unnecessary weight to your pack. We do not recommend such devices for most wilderness navigation.)

Suppose you want to find the distance from Blue Lake to Johnson Mountain as shown in figure 31. You can measure the straight-line distance from the lake's outlet at its southwest tip to the summit of Johnson Mountain to find out how far a trip it would be. If you place the scale of your compass along this route, you can measure this distance in millimeters or inches. Placing the compass along the scales at the bottom of the map shows that this corresponds to about 0.4 mile or 2200 feet (0.7 km or 700 meters).

Note that there is a trail from Blue Lake to the summit of Johnson Mountain. Though the distance to the peak will be longer via the trail, the travel will most certainly be easier. You can measure the distance along the trail by placing the free end of the lanyard on the map at the outlet of Blue Lake, then curving the lanyard along the trail until it reaches the summit of Johnson Mountain. Then straighten out the lanyard and place it alongside whatever scale you want to use at the bottom of the map. The distance corresponds to about 1.3 miles or 7000 feet (2.1 km or 2100 meters).

You can use either feet and miles or meters and kilometers for measuring or pacing distances. However, metric units are much easier to use, since you can easily convert distances in your head from kilometers

Figure 31. Measuring distance and finding elevation gain from a topographic map

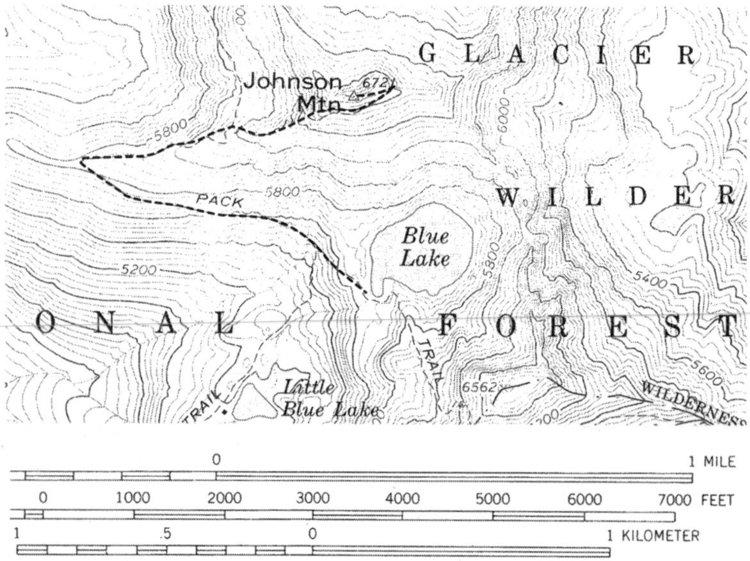

to meters and vice versa, by multiplying or dividing by 1000. Converting miles to feet or vice versa, on the other hand, requires multiplying or dividing by 5280 (the number of feet in a mile), which can be time-consuming and cumbersome in the field. Most wilderness travelers do not wish to carry pocket calculators on their adventures. Also, most countries in the world publish maps based solely on the metric (or International) system, so if you ever travel outside the United States it is good to become accustomed to the metric system. Problems 2, 3, 10, and 11 in the appendix will give you additional practice in measuring distances on a map.

Pace. It is occasionally necessary to go a certain distance in a given direction, for example, 300 feet (100 m) in a northeasterly direction. Doing this requires a good estimate of your pace. All wilderness travelers should have a rough idea of the length of their pace. The length of your normal pace is the distance you cover when you walk two steps (a step with each foot) on level ground at a comfortable walking stride. To measure your normal pace, establish a starting point in an open area where you will be able to walk in a straight line on level terrain. Walk for ten full paces (ten steps with each foot), and mark the place where you stopped. Then measure, with a tape measure in feet or meters, the distance you walked. Divide the distance by ten to get the length of your pace. The normal pace for most people ranges from 3 to 6 feet (1 to 2 m).

Once you know your pace, you can use it to travel a certain distance in the field. Suppose you want to travel 1000 feet, and you know your pace is 5 feet. Divide 1000 feet by 5 feet per pace, and the result is 200 paces. This is easy to do if the numbers are simple, as in this example. If the numbers do not divide evenly, such as when traveling 840 feet with a pace of 5.3 feet, you may need a calculator to figure out the number of paces. It is impractical to carry a calculator on a wilderness trek, so this sort of calculation is best done at home before the trip, as a part of preparing a route plan.

When using the length of pace in your travels, keep in mind that your actual pace will vary considerably due to differences in terrain. For example, your pace will be shorter when going uphill or through heavy brush, and it will probably be longer when descending a good trail. So whenever you use your pace in navigation, be sure to make allowances for variations in the length of your pace with the terrain.

Counting paces is a poor way to travel in the wilderness, since it is easy to lose count. If you concentrate hard enough to avoid losing count, you may miss important details of the route, such as key topographic features, and it may detract from your enjoyment of the trip. Keeping track of your location is far better achieved by watching the topography. If counting paces is necessary at all, we recommend that you use it only for short distances.

SLOPE MEASUREMENT ON THE MAP

By carefully measuring the distance between contour lines on a topographic map, you can estimate the steepness, or *grade*, of the slope as a percentage. This knowledge is important in estimating the risk of avalanches (see "On Snow" in chapter 10) and for determining the feasibility of a particular route. You can do this in the field, but it is easiest if done at home before your trip.

In the example shown in figure 31, we found the straight-line distance from Blue Lake to Johnson Mountain to be about 2200 feet. We can find the grade of this slope by dividing the vertical distance, or elevation gain, by the horizontal distance, and multiplying the result by 100 percent. The elevation of Johnson Mountain is 6721 feet (as shown on the map), and the elevation of Blue Lake is 5625 feet. Subtracting 5625 from 6721 gives an elevation gain of 1096 feet. If you were to travel in a straight line from Blue Lake to Johnson Mountain, the grade of the slope would be the elevation gain (1096 feet) divided by the horizontal distance (2200 feet), multiplied by 100 percent. This gives a grade of about 50 percent, which is a very steep grade; traveling along this route will be difficult and possibly dangerous. Note also that this 50 percent is merely an average grade. The first 200 feet of gain will be rather gentle, but the next 400 feet will be steeper, as can be inferred from the close contour lines. Above 6200 feet, the slope eases up somewhat. Since the average grade is 50 percent and some of the route has a lesser grade, it is apparent that the steepest grade along this route will be even more than 50 percent.

If you instead take the trail from Blue Lake to Johnson Mountain, the elevation gain is the same: 1096 feet. But the distance that you measured earlier using the lanyard of the compass was about 7000 feet. The average grade along the trail is therefore 1096 divided by 7000, multiplied by 100 percent, or about 16 percent. This is a much more reasonable grade than that of the straight-line route, and it will probably be an enjoyable hike rather than a difficult and possibly dangerous climb.

These examples illustrate how to find the average grade over some distance. You can also find the steepest grade along any route using a similar procedure. Draw a line on the map indicating your proposed route. Pick out the place on this line that appears to be the steepest—the place where the contour lines are closest together. Identify two particular contour lines in this area—for example, two index contours (indicated by the heavier contour lines). The difference between these two lines is the vertical height of the slope. Now measure the horizontal distance between these same two lines with the scale of your compass (or any other suitable device). Transfer this measurement to the feet scale at the bottom of the map. Then you can find the steepest grade of the slope by making the same calculation as above.

If you have a metric map, the contour interval will be in meters instead of feet. In this case, your horizontal distance must also be in meters. Use whatever units you want, as long as you use the same for both vertical and horizontal measurements.

Figure 32 shows several examples of measuring the grade of the slope. Points A and B are at elevations of 3600 and 3400 feet, so the vertical height is 3600 minus 3400, or 200 feet. The horizontal distance on the map, which can be measured with a ruler, is found to be 5 centimeters. Transferring this to the scale for feet at the bottom of the map gives a distance of 3800 feet. The grade is 200 feet divided by 3800 feet, multiplied by 100 percent, or 0.05 multiplied by 100 percent, which equals 5 percent.

Figure 32. Measuring grade on a map

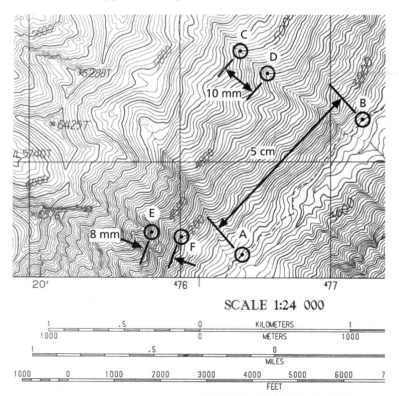

Points C and D in figure 32 are at elevations of 5000 feet and 4600 feet, so the vertical height is 400 feet. The horizontal distance is 10 millimeters, which, when transferred to the scale for feet, gives 800 feet. The grade is 400 feet divided by 800 feet, multiplied by 100 percent, which equals 50 percent.

Points E and F are at elevations of 4800 feet and 4200 feet. The vertical height is 600 feet. The horizontal distance on the map is 8 millimeters, corresponding to a distance of 600 feet, which is the same as the vertical height of 600 feet. The grade is 100 percent—a 45-degree angle.

A grade of 50 percent corresponds to approximately a 27-degree angle. If the vertical height is equal to the horizontal distance, the grade is 100 percent, and the angle of the slope is 45°.

Measuring the grade of the slope is easy; it merely requires dividing the vertical height by the horizontal distance (sometimes called "rise over run"). But expressing the result as an angle, in degrees, requires the use of trigonometry, which we would rather avoid in the field. For your information, the relationship between slope grade and slope angle is shown in the following table:

SLOPE GRADE AND SLOPE ANGLE

% Grade	Angle (in degrees)	% Grade	Angle (in degrees)
0%	0°	90%	42°
10%	6°	100%	45°
20%	11°	120%	50°
30%	17°	140%	54°
40%	22°	170%	60°
50%	27°	200%	63°
60%	31°	250%	68°
70%	35°	300%	72°
80%	39°	400%	76°

You can use this table (or trigonometry if you know it) for trip planning at home, but in the field you usually need to know only a few values. A 20-percent grade is representative of a reasonably steep trail, such as one that gains about 1000 feet in 1 mile. A 50-percent grade has an angle of 27°, a 100-percent grade has an angle of 45°, and a 170-percent grade has an angle of 60°. These four numbers can help you to determine the feasibility of negotiating a particular slope and can also help you to assess the risk of avalanche hazard (see "On Snow" in chapter 10). A 50-percent grade (27-degree angle) is a very steep slope, well past the limit for hiking. Slopes steeper than 50 percent usually involve difficult scrambling or climbing. By the time the grade gets to 100 percent (a 45-degree angle), the terrain is usually too steep for unroped travel, and you will probably need to belay for safety. On snow, you may need an ice ax even if the grade is less than 30 percent. All wilderness travelers should know their limits when it comes to slope. Sometime when you are going up or down a slope that appears to be at your limit, and you feel uncomfortable about being on steeper terrain, mark that spot on your map. Once you get home, measure the grade of that slope on the map as mentioned above. Then you will know your limit, and the next time you contemplate a route in unfamiliar territory, you will be able to measure its grade on the map to find out if it is within your limits.

Problems 5, 6, 13, and 14 in the appendix will give you more practice in measuring slope grade from a map.

RANGE, TOWNSHIP, AND SECTION

The primary surveying system used in most parts of the United States is the range, township, and section system. In this system, most of the United States is divided into regions called *townships*. This system is used in all the states west of the Mississippi River (except for Texas), as well as in Minnesota, Wisconsin, Michigan, Ohio, Indiana, Illinois, Mississippi, Alabama, and Florida.

A township is a 36-square-mile area. The township is divided into thirty-six 1-square-mile *sections*. The sections are numbered from one to thirty-six in a zigzag pattern starting at the northeast corner of the township (see fig. 33).

Each section is divided into quarter-sections, such as the "northeast quarter of section 23." If necessary, these quarter-sections are sometimes further subdivided. In this way, a certain location can be pinpointed to within a small fraction of a mile.

Each township is identified by its location with respect to a *baseline* and a *meridian* in a local coordinate system. One example is the Willamette Baseline and the Principal Willamette Meridian, whose intersection is located near Portland, Oregon.

Special lines are used to divide land areas into these 6-mile squares. These lines are called "township lines" and "range lines." Township lines run east and west, and are numbered based on their distance north or south of the baseline. Range lines run north and south, and are numbered based on their distance east or west of the principal meridian.

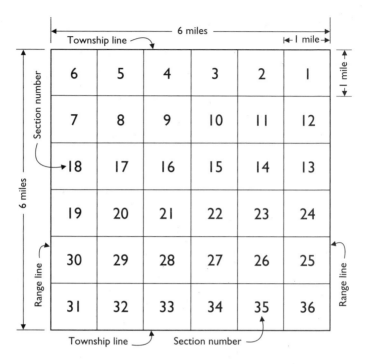

Figure 33. A township consists of an area 6 miles on a side and contains 36 sections. A section is a square 1 mile on each side.

The location of each township in the states of Washington and Oregon is referred to by its distance from the intersection of the Principal Willamette Meridian and the Willamette Baseline (see fig. 34). A township whose northern boundary is three township lines (18 miles) north of the Willamette Baseline is identified as T3N. If this area's eastern boundary is five range lines (30 miles) east of the Principal Willamette Meridian, the township is identified with the designation R5E. If a specific location within this township is in Section 23, then the section is identified as Section 23, Township 3N, Range 5E, or Section 23, T3N, R5E.

In locations where the land has been surveyed using this method, the boundaries between sections, ranges, and township lines are usually indicated by light red lines on USGS topographic maps. The township and range boundaries are shown by red letters and numbers such as R5E or T6N near the edges of the maps. The sections are numbered from 1 to 36 with red numbers in the centers of the sections. In figure 35,

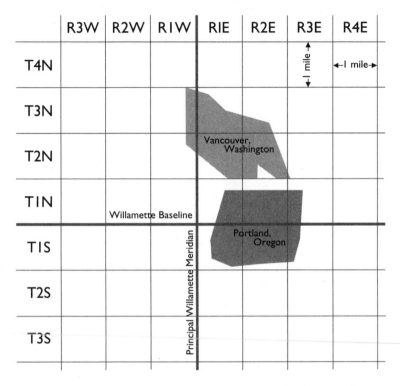

Figure 34. In the states of Washington and Oregon, township line boundaries are defined based on the distances north and south of the Willamette Baseline. Range line boundaries are defined based on the distances east and west of the Principal Willamette Meridian. These two lines intersect just west of Portland, Oregon.

for example, the hill indicated by A is in Section 36, T15N, R6E. Big Creek Campground (indicated by B) is in Section 6, T14N, R7E.

Some areas in the United States have not yet been surveyed. In these areas, the range, township, and section system cannot be used. In this case, locations can be specified using the latitude/longitude system or the Universal Transverse Mercator (UTM) system. The use of the UTM system will be explained in greater detail in chapter 9, since it is of particular interest to users of GPS receivers.

Most law enforcement agencies and search and rescue organizations are very familiar with the range, township, and section method. When communicating with such agencies or organizations, the best system to identify such an area has usually been the range, township, and section method. However, due to increasing use of the GPS, many search and rescue organizations and governmental agencies are presently using either latitude/longitude or the UTM system for defining position. For this reason it is good to be familiar with all three systems.

Figure 35. A portion of a USGS topographic map, showing section, range, and township numbers and boundaries

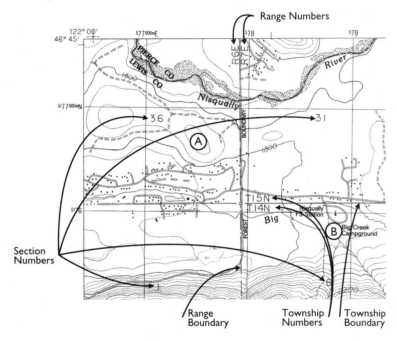

Chapter
7

More about Compasses and Geomagnetism

Chapter 2 provided a general introduction to the subject of compasses, explained how to use a compass to take and follow bearings in the field, and how to measure and plot bearings on a map. This chapter goes deeper into the subject of compass use by providing detailed information on how to get accurate declination information. It also gives an explanation of how and why declination is changing and how to deal with these changes. In addition, it provides information regarding compass dip, using the compass clinometer, and using Brunton compasses, which was not covered in chapter 2.

WHERE TO GET DECLINATION INFORMATION

To find the declination for any point in the United States, call the USGS at (303) 273-8487. For Canada, call the Geological Survey of Canada at (613) 837-4241.

Declination information is also available on the Internet. The National Oceanographic and Atmospheric Agency (NOAA) website, *www.ngdc.noaa.gov/seg/geomag/declination.shtml,* provides declination information for any place in the United States with only the postal ZIP code or the latitude/longitude coordinates of the location. The latter can be found by looking at any corner of a USGS topographic map for the area of interest. In addition to giving the magnetic declination in degrees, this website provides the present amount of annual change in declination in minutes (1/60 of a degree) and provides declination maps of the contiguous United States and the world. The default latitude and longitude are north latitude and west longitude, which is appropriate for the United States, Canada, and Mexico. It is possible, however, to enter southern latitudes and eastern longitudes, and therefore to find the declination for any point on the surface of the earth. For example, the coordinates for Melbourne, Australia, are 38° S latitude and 145° E longitude. The NOAA website gives a declination of 11°43' E (approximately 12° E) for this location for the year 2004.

Another useful website is the Canadian Geomagnetic Reference Field (CGRF), *www.geolab.nrcan.gc.ca/geomag/mirp_e.shtml*. This will give you present declination for anywhere in North America when you enter a set of latitude and longitude coordinates. The CGRF can also give you declination for any year from 1960 to 2005; this time span is increased as time progresses.

The CGRF is specifically designed for use in Canada, but it works just as well for the United States. The CGRF data input assumes that all latitudes are north and all longitudes are west. However, if you enter negative values of latitude or longitude, it is possible to obtain declination information for any place in the world. Using the Melbourne, Australia, example again with a latitude of 38° S and longitude 145° E, you can enter a latitude of -38° N and a longitude of -145° W. The result, for the year 2004, is 11°43' E, just as with the NOAA website.

Both of the above-mentioned websites provide additional interesting and useful information on declination and compass use.

In most parts of the world, you can buy topographic maps with declination information. If you go somewhere where you cannot find the declination, and if you do not have access to a computer, you can find a fairly close estimate of the declination from figure 36.

CHANGES IN DECLINATION

Magnetic declination is caused by the motion of magnetic material in the earth's core. The dirt and rock upon which we live is only a relatively thin crust. Beneath this is a solid *mantle* of rock extending to a depth of about 1800 miles. Beneath this is a molten interior more than a thousand miles thick. In the center of the earth there is a solid inner core, rotating at a slightly different rate than the outer mantle. This rotational motion causes the molten material between the two solid portions to move. Since this material is magnetic in nature (predominantly iron), its constant motion creates a slowly varying magnetic field.

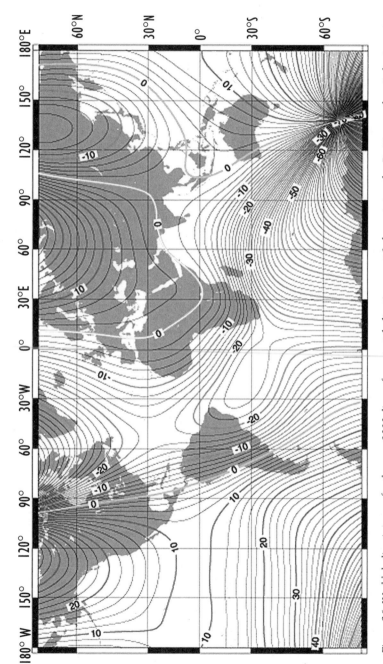

Figure 36. World declination map for the year 2000: lines of constant declination are at 2-degree intervals. Positive numbers indicate east declination; negative numbers indicate west declination.

The motion of the molten magnetic material is mostly random and unpredictable, so we cannot predict with certainty what the declination will be at any given place at some future time. However, the earth is very large, and changes take place slowly. Declination and its rate of change can be studied and recorded over long periods of time to arrive at mathematical models that predict declination over a relatively short period of time, such as a few years. This is the basis for the declination prediction models referred to above.

Figure 37 is a map of the continental United States with annual declination changes over the past half century shown by curved lines. The zero change line runs through the southern part of Maine. This means that declination has hardly been changing at all in areas near this line. The declination given on a map dated 1960 to 2000 for an area in Maine or New Hampshire will probably be fairly accurate until at least 2010.

A line representing a declination change of 0.1° westward per year runs roughly through Seattle, Helena, Kansas City, Little Rock, and New Orleans. Therefore, declination along this line has been changing by about 0.1° per year, or 1° per decade. If you have an old map stating that the declination in some area along or near this line was 22° E in 1964, you can find its declination for the year 2004 by finding the difference in years: 2004 minus 1964 equals 40 years. Multiply 40 years by 0.1° per year and you get a change of 4°. This change is westward, and the stated declination is east, so you must subtract the 4-degree change from the old 22° E value to arrive at 18° E in 2004.

Another line along which the declination change has been 0.1° westward per year is close to Marquette in Michigan's Upper Peninsula, Columbus, and Raleigh. But the declination in these areas is west, so the declination change has to be *added* in these areas east of the zero declination line. For example, suppose you have a 1934 map for the area near Columbus, Ohio, which states its magnetic declination as 1° W. Figure 37 indicates that the declination change has been 0.1° westward per year. To find the declination for the year 2004, subtract 1934 from 2004 and get 70 years. Multiply 70 years by 0.1° per year to get 7°. Add this to the 1934 declination of 1° W and the result is 8° W for 2004. This is reasonably close to the value shown in the U.S. declination map (fig. 10) in chapter 2.

Figure 37 also shows the declination change for Alaska. Note that in extreme northeastern Alaska, the declination change has been nearly 0.2° westward per year, or nearly 1° every five years.

Throughout the Hawaiian Islands, the declination change has been about 0.06° westward per year.

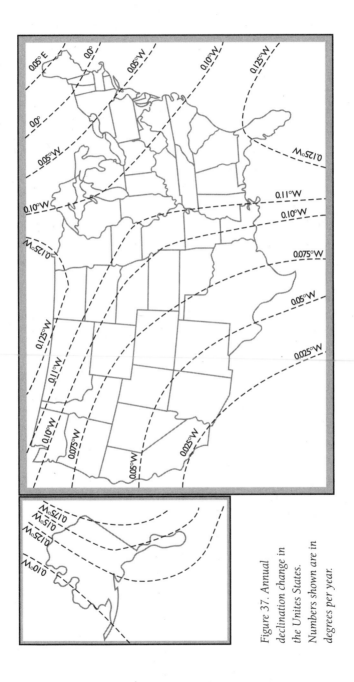

Figure 37. Annual declination change in the Unites States. Numbers shown are in degrees per year.

Recent observations indicate that the amount of declination change is increasing in some areas and decreasing in others. Therefore, using figure 37 for five or more years in the future might not be very accurate for some locations. Our intent in showing figure 37 is to allow you to correct the declination given on older maps. The actual date for the data in figure 37 is 1990. This date makes it most accurate for converting a declination on a map dated 1975 to a value for the year 2005. However, it can be used with reasonable accuracy to correct any map dated 1950 or later to its present-time value (2000 to 2010).

DIP

The magnetic needle of the compass is not only affected by the horizontal direction of the earth's magnetic field but also by its vertical pull. The closer you get to the magnetic north pole, the more the north-seeking end of the needle tends to point *downward*. At the magnetic equator, the needle will be level, while at the south magnetic pole the north-seeking end of the needle tries to point in an *upward* direction. This phenomenon is referred to as compass *dip*. To compensate for this effect, most compass manufacturers purposely introduce a slight imbalance to the magnetic needles of their compasses, so that their dip is negligible for the geographic area where they will be used. The earth is divided into dip zones, and compasses sold in each zone are compensated for use in that zone.

If you buy a compass in one dip zone and try to use it in another, the compass may not work well because of the difference in dip. For example, if you buy a compass in North America or Europe and then try to use it in Argentina, New Zealand, or some other place in the southern hemisphere, the difference in dip may be enough to introduce errors in your compass readings or even make the compass impossible to use. For this reason, if you bring your compass to a faraway place, you should first try it out in an urban area as soon as you arrive, to make sure it works properly before heading out into the wilderness. If it is adversely affected by dip, you may have to buy a new compass in the general area where you will be traveling.

Some manufacturers produce compasses that are not affected by dip. These compasses have the term "global" in their names, or a notation on the package that the compass is corrected for dip anywhere in the world. If you intend to go on worldwide adventures, you might consider such a compass.

Another way of ensuring that your compass will not be affected by dip is to buy one ahead of time that is properly compensated for dip in the area you will be visiting. Some retail stores and mail-order companies have, or can order, compasses compensated for whatever zone you will be visiting.

USING THE CLINOMETER

Some compasses are equipped with clinometers, which measure angles of slope. To use the clinometer on your compass, set either 90° or 270° at the index line. Hold the compass with its long edge horizontal, so that the clinometer needle points down toward the numbered scale (which may be the same scale used for declination adjustment). With the direction-of-travel line horizontal, the clinometer should read zero. Tilting the compass up or down will cause the clinometer needle to point to the number of degrees upward or downward.

There are two ways to use the clinometer. The first is to measure the angle to a distant object. For example, suppose you are at the summit of a peak, and you see another peak of nearly the same elevation. You wonder if you are on the higher of the two summits. Hold the compass with its long edge pointing toward the other peak, as you sight along the long edge of the base plate (see fig. 38). Steady the compass on a rock or other stable object if possible. Tap the compass lightly to overcome any friction in the mechanism, and ask a companion to look at the clinometer needle from the side to see if it indicates an upward or a downward angle toward the other peak. Or you can read the angle to the object yourself by folding the mirror at a 45-degree angle, sighting along the edge of the base plate at the object, and reading the upward or downward angle in the mirror. If it indicates an upward angle, then the other peak is higher than you are. Sorry.

Figure 38. Using a clinometer to find the angle of elevation of a distant object

Figure 39. Using a clinometer to find the angle of slope at some particular point

The clinometer can also be used to find the angle of the slope. In chapter 6, you learned how to determine the angle of slope from a map. The clinometer, however, can tell you the actual angle of the slope on which you are standing. As above, set 90° or 270° at the index line, and then lay the long edge of the compass on the slope (fig. 39). Read the angle of slope on the clinometer scale. Due to variations in the slope over small distances, it is best to place an ice ax, a branch, a ski pole, or some other long object along the slope, and then place the long edge of the compass along this object to get a better idea of the average slope. The presence of metal, such as an ice ax or ski pole shaft, will affect the magnetic needle but not the clinometer needle, which works with gravity.

OTHER TYPES OF COMPASSES

Base plate compasses, such as Silva, Suunto, Nexus, and some others are similar to the models shown in figure 5, and the methods of using these compasses are as described in chapter 2. Several Brunton base plate compasses, which work differently from those mentioned above are also available, and are also acceptable for use in wilderness navigation.

Most Brunton compasses (except for the Nexus and Eclipse models) have adjustable declination arrows, but there is no screwdriver adjustment as with other compasses. Instead, Bruntons have a round capsule within the rotating housing. To adjust for declination, you lightly squeeze this capsule between your thumb and forefinger while you grasp the rotating housing with your other hand. Then you turn the capsule to point the declination arrow to the correct number of degrees, as shown in figure 40 (for example, 12° in Arizona, or 345° in Vermont, for a declination of 15° W). The compass is then used in the same way as other compasses described in chapter 2.

Since Brunton compasses have no meridian lines in the transparent capsule, the procedure for measuring and plotting bearings on maps is also slightly different. Bruntons have partial meridian lines, aligned with north and south on the dial, on the outer ring of the rotating housing. To measure or plot bearings on a map, follow the procedures described earlier for other compasses, except that you should align the partial meridian lines on the outside ring with the north-south lines on the map. As with the other compasses, always make sure that the N on the rotating compass dial is aligned toward north (usually the top) of the

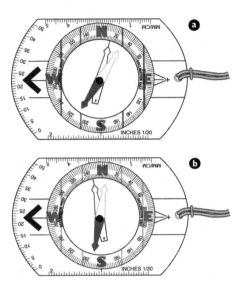

Figure 40. Adjusting a Brunton 9020 compass for declination: a. Arizona, 12° E, b. Vermont, 15° W

map. In figure 41, a Brunton 9020 compass is being used to measure the bearing from point A to point B on a map. The partial meridian lines on the rotating housing are aligned with the meridian lines on the map, and you can see the result (320°) at the index line.

The Brunton Eclipse compass is excellent for wilderness navigation. You can adjust it for declination by turning the compass over and finding a declination scale. By holding the compass capsule with the fingers of one hand and turning the compass dial with the other, you turn the capsule until the blue arrow points to the correct east or west declination. The compass is then boxed by getting the red N circle inside the open blue circle. The Eclipse models have partial meridian lines on the outside ring, just as the Brunton 9020. Therefore, to measure or plot bearings on a map, use the same procedures as stated above for the Brunton 9020.

Some base plate compasses have rotating housings that are marked from 0° to 90° and back to 0°, and then to 90° and back to 0° again. These are called *quadrant* types, and some people prefer them. Bearings taken with a quadrant compass are often expressed as the number of degrees east or west of north or south. For example, S 20° E, which means 20° east of south, or 180° minus 20° equals 160°. We do not recommend these for wilderness navigation, since using

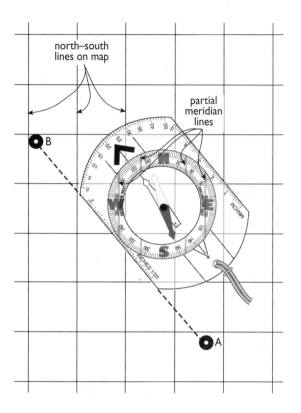

Figure 41. Using a Brunton 9020 compass to measure a bearing on a map

them requires the use of mental arithmetic—and you know what we think of *that*.

For wilderness travel we recommend base plate compasses. And all of the examples of taking, following, measuring, and plotting bearings are based on the assumption that you are using such a compass. Most of the compasses listed in chapter 2 are marked to 2-degree divisions, and it is unlikely that you can achieve better accuracy than that with those compasses. Many people have difficulty obtaining better than 5° accuracy using compasses without a mirror. Even with a mirror, it is difficult to get accuracy consistently better than 2°. There are, however, other more precise compasses, most notably optical sighting compasses, such as the Plastimo Iris 50; the Weems & Plath Hand Bearing compass; the Vion Mini 2000; the Suunto KB-14/360, KB-14/360D, KB-20, and KB-77; the Brunton Sight Master; and others.

There are even battery-operated digital compasses such as the Brunton NOMAD digital compass. These are more accurate and more precise than most base plate compasses and are useful if the accuracy you need is not possible with a base plate compass. Some, such as the Brunton NOMAD and the Suunto KB-14/360D, have adjustable declination. Most of the others do not, so you may need to add or subtract declination (as described in chapter 2). Most of these are not base plate compasses, so in order to use any of these with a map, you also need to bring along a protractor, or a base plate compass to measure and plot bearings.

One particularly interesting optical sighting compass is the Brunton 54LU Combi, which is an optical sighting base plate compass that also works in a non-optical sighting mode. You can correct it for declination by using a taped declination arrow, as described in chapter 2, but this only works for the non-optical mode. To take advantage of the added accuracy provided by the optical mode (with 1-degree resolution), you have to add or subtract declination. But since it is a base plate compass, you can use it for measuring and plotting bearings on a map, unlike most other optical sighting compasses.

Base plate compasses can be found at most outdoor recreation stores, while nautical supply stores usually carry optical sighting compasses. In addition, several mail-order companies sell compasses, altimeters, GPS receivers, and other equipment of interest to the wilderness traveler. Two of these are the Ben Meadows Company (1-800-241-6401; *www.benmeadows.com*) and Forestry Suppliers, Inc. (1-800-647-5368; *www.forestry-suppliers.com*). You can also check out the variety of compasses available at some compass manufacturers' websites, such as *www.brunton.com, www.silvacompass.com,* and *www.suunto.com.*

Chapter 8

The Altimeter

The altimeter, like a compass, provides one simple piece of information that forms the basis for a tremendous amount of vital detail: *elevation*. By monitoring the elevation and checking it against the topographic map, wilderness travelers can keep track of their progress, pinpoint their location, and find their way to critical junctions on the route. In mountainous terrain, the altimeter can be a great help in orientation, navigation, and routefinding.

WHAT THE ALTIMETER IS AND HOW IT WORKS

An altimeter is basically a modified barometer. Both instruments measure air pressure (the weight of air). A barometer measures air pressure on a scale calibrated in inches of mercury, or in millibars. An altimeter measures air pressure on a scale calibrated in feet or meters above or below sea level; air pressure changes at a predictable rate with changing altitude.

TYPES OF ALTIMETERS

The most popular type of wilderness altimeter is the digital wristwatch combination (fig. 42a and 42b). The digital wristwatch altimeter has several advantages over the analog type (fig. 42c). Some digital altimeters display additional information, such as the temperature and the rate of altitude gain or loss. Since most people wear a watch anyway, this type of altimeter is helpful because it combines multiple functions into one piece of equipment. The altimeter worn on the wrist is more convenient and therefore will be consulted more frequently than one kept in a pocket or pack.

A disadvantage of the digital altimeter is that it requires a battery that can die out or become temporarily disconnected due to mechanical shock, causing all of its data to be lost. It can also fail if water gets into the mechanism. The liquid crystal display (LCD) usually goes blank at temperatures below about 0°F (-18°C), making it essential to

Figure 42. Typical altimeters: a, b digital wristwatch types, c analog pocket type

keep the instrument relatively warm. (This is usually not a problem as long as you keep the altimeter on your wrist. If it gets cold enough for the LCD to go blank, the altimeter will still retain all of its data and will display the data properly once it warms up enough for the display to work.) When starting a technical rock-climbing pitch, it is a good idea to remove the altimeter from your wrist and attach it to your pack's shoulder strap, or put in into your pack or pocket to keep it from getting banged up on the rock or stuck in a crack.

The analog altimeter has the advantages of being a simpler instrument: it requires no battery and continues to display the elevation even at temperatures well below zero. To read an analog altimeter, hold it level in the palm of your hand. Look directly down on the needle, your eyes at least a foot (30 cm) above it, to reduce errors due to viewing angle. Tap it lightly several times to overcome any slight friction in the mechanism.

EFFECTS OF WEATHER ON ALTIMETERS

The accuracy of an altimeter depends on the weather, because a change in the weather is usually accompanied by a change in air pressure, which causes an error in the altimeter reading. A change in barometric pressure of 1 inch of mercury corresponds to a change in altitude of roughly 1000 feet. (A pressure change of 10 millibars corresponds to about 100 meters of elevation change.)

If you are in camp during a day in which the air pressure increases by two-tenths of an inch of mercury, or about 6 millibars, (for example, from 30.00 to 30.20 inches, or from 1016 to 1022 millibars), your altimeter will show a reading about 200 feet (60 m) less than it was at the beginning of the day, even though you have remained in the same place. If you had gone out on a hike during that same day, your elevation readings by the end of the day would likewise have been about 200 feet (60 m) too low. During periods of unstable weather, the elevation indicated on your altimeter may change by as much as 500 feet (150 m) in one day even though your actual elevation has remained the same. Even during apparently stable conditions, an erroneous indicated change in elevation of 100 feet (30 m) per day is not uncommon.

PRECISION AND ACCURACY

Because even the most precise and costly altimeters are strongly influenced by the weather, do not be misled into trusting them to a degree of accuracy that is greater than possible. A typical high-quality altimeter may have a precision (smallest marked division of an analog instrument, or smallest indicated change of a digital one) of 10 feet (3 m) or even less. This does not mean the altimeter will always be that accurate. Changes in weather could easily throw its reading off by hundreds of feet or meters.

EFFECTS OF TEMPERATURE ON ALTIMETERS

The altimeter sensor expands and contracts due to variations in temperature, causing changes in the indicated elevation. A bimetallic element in *temperature-compensated* altimeters adjusts for this effect *when there is no actual change in elevation.* When you are gaining or losing elevation, however, this compensation is sometimes not enough, resulting in errors even in temperature-compensated altimeters. To minimize the effects of temperature changes, try to keep the altimeter's temperature as constant as possible. Body heat will usually accomplish this with a wristwatch altimeter, particularly if it is worn under a parka when the outside temperature is low. With an analog altimeter, you can keep its temperature relatively constant by carrying it in your pocket rather than in your pack.

CAUTIONS WHEN USING THE ALTIMETER IN WILDERNESS TRAVEL

Because of the strong influence of weather on an altimeter's accuracy, you cannot trust the instrument until you first set it at a known elevation, such as a trailhead. Then it is important, when you are traveling, to check the reading whenever you reach other points of known elevation, so you can reset it if necessary or at least be aware of the error. Get to know your altimeter, use it often, check it at every opportunity, and note differences of opinion between it and the map. You will soon learn just what level of accuracy to expect, and your altimeter will become a dependable aid to roving the wilds.

ORIENTATION

An altimeter can be a big help in determining exactly where you are. If you are climbing a ridge or hiking up a trail shown on the map, but you do not know exactly where you are along the ridge or trail, check the altimeter for the elevation. Where the ridge or trail reaches that contour line on the map is your likely location.

Another way to use the altimeter to determine where you are is to start with a compass bearing to a summit or some other known feature. Find that peak on the map and plot the bearing line from the mountain back toward your approximate location. This gives you line position; you know you must be somewhere along this line. But where? Look at your altimeter for the elevation reading. Your likely location is where the compass bearing line crosses a contour line at this elevation. This could lead to an ambiguous answer, of course, because the bearing line might cross that contour line at several points. Then turn to further observations (such as slope direction, topography, and vegetation), common sense, and intuition.

Problems 21 and 27 in the appendix involve orientation using a map and altimeter readings.

NAVIGATION

Navigation becomes easier with an altimeter. If you top a convenient couloir at 9400 feet (2870 m) and gain the ridge you want to ascend, make a note of that elevation in a notebook or on the map. On your return, descend the ridge to that elevation, and you should easily find the couloir again.

Guidebook descriptions sometimes specify a change of direction at a particular elevation. If you are on an open snowfield or a forested hillside, good luck in making the turn at the right place without an altimeter. The route you have worked out on a topographic map also may depend on course changes at certain elevations, and again the altimeter will keep your party on target.

DECISION MAKING

The altimeter can help you to decide whether to continue a trip or to turn back by letting you calculate your rate of ascent. Suppose you have been keeping an hourly check on time and elevation during a climb. It has taken the party 4 hours to ascend 3000 feet (910 m), an average of 750 feet (230 m) per hour. But you know that the actual rate of ascent has been declining with each hour. In fact, the party gained only 500 feet (150 m) in the past hour, compared with 1000 feet (300 m) in the first hour. You know that the destination is at an elevation of 8400 feet (2560 m), and an altimeter reading shows you are now at 6400 feet (1950 m). You can therefore predict that it will take roughly 4 more hours to reach your destination. Take that information, courtesy of the altimeter, combine it with a look at the weather, the time of the day, and the condition of party members, and you have the data on which to base a sound decision as to whether to proceed with the trip or turn back.

Predicting the Weather

The altimeter can help in predicting the weather. The readings on an altimeter and on a barometer operate in opposition to one another. When one goes up, the other goes down. An altimeter reading that shows an increase in elevation when no actual elevation change has taken place (such as at camp overnight) means a falling barometer, which often predicts deteriorating weather. An altimeter reading that shows a decrease, on the other hand, means increasing barometric pressure and possibly improving weather. This is an oversimplification, of course; weather forecasting is complicated by the wind, local weather peculiarities, and the rate of barometric pressure change. Make frequent observations of altimeter readings and weather patterns on your trips—and even while at home—if you want to figure out the relationship between weather and altimeter readings in your particular geographic area.

Some digital wristwatch altimeters can be set to read barometric pressure instead of altitude. But keep in mind that changes in barometric pressure are useful in assessing the weather only when the readings are taken at a constant elevation (such as in camp). Using the altimeter as a barometer while you are ascending or descending will give readings that are influenced not only by changes in barometric pressure but also by changes in your elevation as you travel. Your conclusions about barometric pressure trends may be erroneous under such circumstances.

On extended trips, it is often a good idea to keep track of barometric pressure trends at camps. Be sure to reset the altimeter at known elevations, then record pressure or altitude readings in your notebook or journal, along with notes about weather conditions, such as whether it is raining, snowing, windy, sunny, etc. By documenting pressure trends and weather patterns, you will learn how to predict future weather based on past observations. This works best at fixed camps at known elevations.

USE OF BEARING OF THE SLOPE WITH THE ALTIMETER

The *bearing of the slope* (described in chapter 3) becomes a very powerful tool when combined with altimeter use. Sometimes, when on a featureless snow slope, in a dense forest, or in foggy conditions, it is impossible to take bearings on visible landmarks, and there are no identifiable topographic features for you to compare to the map. Under these and similar conditions, knowing your altitude plus the bearing of the slope can often provide enough information to enable you to determine your position with a high degree of certainty. In fact, in the absence of definite topographic features or visible landmarks, the use of the altimeter plus the bearing of the slope might well be the *only* way to determine your position, unless you have a GPS receiver.

The Global Positioning System

Note: If you skipped all the other chapters and turned to this one first, thinking that using the global positioning system (GPS) will make it unnecessary for you to learn map and compass, please **go back** to the beginning of the book and read at least chapters 1 through 5 before reading this chapter. Using GPS technology effectively requires a basic understanding of how to read maps and how to use a compass.

The U.S. Department of Defense has placed a system of twenty-four satellites (plus a few spares) in orbit around Earth. GPS receivers (fig. 43) pick up signals from some of these satellites and can give the user's position and altitude to within about 50 feet (15 m), under ideal conditions. In the past (until May 1, 2000) the Department of Defense degraded this accuracy to prevent its use by perceived enemies. This degradation was called *selective availability* (SA). When SA was in effect, GPS point position accuracy was degraded by approximately 300 feet (roughly 100 m). The Department of Defense still has the capability to reinstate SA at any time in the interest of national security, but it is unlikely that this will ever happen, since so many people now depend on accurate GPS usage.

SELECTING A GPS RECEIVER

Most GPS receivers cost from $100 to $400, are about the size of a TV remote control unit, and weigh less than one pound (1/2 kg). Most operate on two or four AA batteries, with a battery life of ten to thirty-six hours, depending on the model. They have a variety of features

Figure 43. Different types of GPS receivers

that allow them to store and later recall specific positions (called *landmarks* or *waypoints*), determine the compass bearing and the distance between waypoints, and plot out routes comprising a series of waypoints from one position to another.

If you decide to buy a GPS receiver, first talk to friends and acquaintances who already own GPS receivers to learn about and compare features, ease of operation, ability to work in challenging terrain, and other attributes. If possible, borrow a receiver and try it out to determine if it is the right receiver for you. If you intend to use it in a cold climate, pay particular attention to the operating temperature limitations stated in its specifications. Some operate reliably only down to freezing; others work to near 0°F (-18°C). Make sure your chosen GPS receiver can make use of the UTM coordinate system (described later in this chapter). Before buying a GPS receiver, take a good look at its instruction manual. If it becomes apparent that you will not be able to understand how to use the instrument, then check out other models that are more user-friendly and easier to operate. Some receivers are designed to make use of two additional satellites that comprise the Wide Area Augmentation System (WAAS), resulting in even greater accuracy—as close as 10 feet (3 meters), under ideal conditions. Much useful information on GPS receivers is available on websites, such as *www.magellangps.com*, *www.garmin.com*, and *www.brunton.com*.

GETTING STARTED WITH GPS
Avoid the temptation to rush out into the wilderness, get lost, and trust that this marvelous electronic gadget will magically get you home

again. Instead, sit down in a comfortable chair and read the instruction manual to become thoroughly familiar with the receiver before using it in the wilderness. (This chapter is intended only as a supplement to the instruction manual that comes with your GPS receiver.) Once you are familiar with your GPS receiver, the first step is to initialize it using a menu-driven set of commands to establish your approximate position. Then select which units to use (miles or kilometers, feet or meters, magnetic or true bearings, etc.) and—very important—select the datum to agree with the topographic map of the area (more about this later in this chapter). If you are using the compass methods described in this book, be sure to use true bearings (usually the default north reference setting) rather than magnetic bearings. Try out the receiver around home, in city parks, and on easy trail hikes before taking it into the wilderness.

USING A GPS RECEIVER IN WILDERNESS NAVIGATION

The first rule of the GPS receiver is not to become dependent on it. It is best to consider the GPS receiver as an extra navigational tool, as a useful addition to a paper map and a magnetic compass, rather than as a replacement for them. If conditions warrant, carry route-marking materials, such as flagging and wands, regardless of whether or not you have a GPS receiver. Never rely solely on a GPS receiver.

A GPS receiver can be used along with a compass in order to be sure you can get back to your starting point. At the trailhead or campsite, or wherever you start your trip, turn on the receiver to establish your GPS position. This usually takes several minutes. Save this position as a waypoint, even giving it a unique name if desired. Then turn off the receiver to save battery power, and pack it away carefully to protect it from harm while you are traveling. Along the route, you may encounter crucial locations, such as important trail junctions, the point where you reach a ridge crest, the point where you left a trail, etc. At such points, turn on the receiver to establish additional waypoints. Once you are at your destination or turnaround point, use the receiver to find the distance and compass bearing from one waypoint to another to return to the starting point. Then turn off the receiver and use your compass to travel to the next waypoint. At any point at which you turn on the receiver and get a position, you can ask the receiver to GO TO the name of any previously stored waypoint. The receiver will then provide the distance and compass bearing to that waypoint.

Many GPS instruction manuals seem to assume that you are always traveling with the receiver turned on and in your hand, constantly observing its display. Doing this wastes battery power and occupies a hand that might be better used for climbing, scrambling, or holding an ice ax or a ski pole. In addition, it distracts you from observing the route, its hazards, and the scenery, and it looks really nerdy. The most efficient way to use a GPS receiver is to use it only occasionally and to travel by compass the rest of the time.

Under some conditions it might be advantageous to leave a GPS receiver turned on for hours at a time while you travel—such as when you are descending through the forest, down a snow slope in a whiteout, or when it is late and darkness is approaching. Under such conditions, every minute might count, making it inconvenient to stop for a few minutes every now and then to allow the receiver to reacquire the position.

If you leave your receiver on as you approach your destination, it will record your route. Then on your return trip you can use the receiver's backtrack mode to retrace your steps very closely. This feature can only be used if you leave the receiver on the entire time en route to your destination, as well as on the return trip.

If you want to leave the receiver turned on under such conditions, find a way to securely attach it to your pack strap or some other easily accessible place so your hands are free while you travel. Then you can look at the receiver any time you want, and you will not have to wait for it to get a position fix.

Be sure to start each full-day or weekend trip with a fresh set of batteries, and consider carrying spare batteries. Be prepared for conditions under which the receiver might not work, such as an electronic failure, topographic or forest features that block the satellite signals, or subfreezing temperatures that might cause the LCD screen to go blank. You could also lose it or drop it. These and other conditions can render your receiver useless, so it is essential to avoid becoming dependent on your GPS receiver.

GPS receivers have some obvious advantages over magnetic compasses. A compass can tell you your position only if you can see landmarks and can take bearings on them. The GPS receiver, on the other hand, can provide your position (usually to within a sphere of uncertainty smaller than the size of a tennis court) *without any visible landmarks* (under ideal conditions). This can be particularly helpful in fog or a whiteout or in featureless terrain.

In chapter 4 we described various strategies to use to follow a compass bearing toward your objective, such as the use of intermediate objectives and detouring a paced distance around an obstruction. When using a compass, such techniques are essential in order to stay on your correct course. With a GPS receiver, however, navigation becomes easier. If you are trying to follow a given bearing to your destination and the route is blocked, you can simply travel around the blockage by the easiest route without worrying about how far off route you get or in what direction. Once past the obstruction, you can again turn on your GPS receiver and obtain a new position. The receiver can then provide the new bearing to your objective, and you can set the new bearing on your compass and follow it.

When planning a wilderness trip, you should find the coordinates of critical sites (e.g., the starting point, the destination, and other crucial points) on the map and enter them into the GPS receiver as waypoints. This can easily be done at home before the trip.

ORIENTATION USING GPS AND UTM COORDINATES

Suppose you want to identify your point position on a map. Take out the GPS receiver, turn it on, and let it acquire a good, stable position. The receiver will probably be reading latitude/longitude coordinates unless you have programmed it otherwise. (Most rescue and military agencies use this system.) For wilderness use, however, the Universal Transverse Mercator (UTM) is a much easier system to use. The UTM system is a grid of north-south and east-west lines at intervals of 1000 meters (3281 ft or 0.62 mile). This is far more precise than the latitude/longitude system, because USGS maps only identify latitude and longitude coordinates every 2.5 minutes—approximately 2 to 3 miles (3 to 4 km). Using the receiver's setup screen, you should be able to change the coordinate system from latitude/longitude to UTM. You can then correlate the UTM numbers on the receiver's screen with the UTM grid on the map. Without using a scale or ruler, you can usually eyeball your position to within about 100 meters (about 300 ft), which is often close enough to get to within sight of your objective. If greater precision is desired, you can use the meters scale at the bottom of the map.

For example, suppose you are climbing Glacier Peak, and clouds obscure all visibility. You reach a summit but are not sure whether it is the true summit of Glacier Peak. Turn on your GPS receiver and let it acquire a position. The UTM numbers on the screen of your GPS receiver are as follows:

10 6 40 612E
53 29 491N

The top number is called an *easting*, which indicates the number of meters east of a reference line for your area. The "10" is the UTM zone number, which you can find in the lower left-hand corner of a USGS topographic map (see fig. 44). The numbers "6 40 612E" indicate that your position is 640,612 meters east of a reference line for your area. In figure 45, you can find the number "6 40 000mE" along the top edge of the map. This is the *full easting* (except for the zone number). To the right of this is the number 6 41. This is a *partial easting*, with the "000" meters omitted. You can see that the number "10 6 40 612E" on the screen of the GPS receiver is approximately six-tenths of the way between 6 40 000 and 6 41 000. Your east-west position is therefore about six-tenths of the way between the 6 40 000 and 6 41 000 lines.

Figure 44. Lower left corner of a USGS topographic map showing UTM zone and horizontal datum. UTM partial eastings and northings also shown.

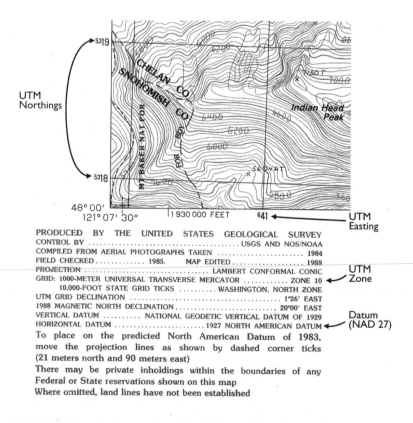

Along the left edge of the map is the number "53 31 000mN". This is the *full northing,* which indicates that this point is 5,331,000 meters north of the equator. Below this is a line labeled "53 30", and another labeled "53 29." These are *partial northings,* with the "000" meters omitted. The lower number displayed on the GPS receiver is 53 29 491N. This is a horizontal line about halfway between 53 29 and 53 30. The point where the easting and the northing lines intersect is your *point position.* Finding this point in figure 45 shows that you are on Disappointment Peak. Bummer.

If you have difficulty eyeballing distances between UTM coordinate lines, there are several types of special rulers and other measuring devices that you can use instead. You can purchase small plastic scales to read UTM coordinates on 1:24,000-scale (7.5-minute) maps, but this means carrying one more piece of special equipment. Some compasses are equipped with special scales to locate your position on 1:24,000 maps; some of these have "GPS" in their model numbers. Other compasses have "roamer" (sometimes spelled "romer") scales for

Figure 45. Example of orientation and navigation using GPS

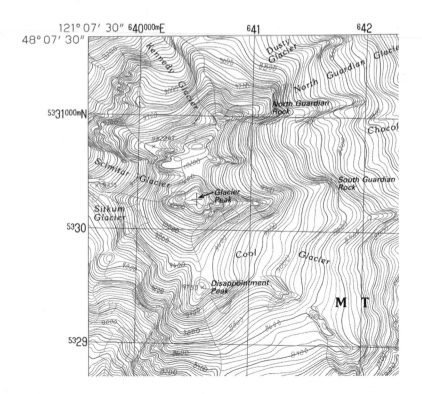

use with either 1:24,000 or 1:25,000 scale maps; since USGS 7.5-minute maps have a scale of 1:24,000, that is the scale you should use. However, if your compass has a roamer scale for use with 1:25,000 maps, it is close enough to 1:24,000 that you can use it anyway, with only minimal error.

NAVIGATION USING GPS AND UTM COORDINATES

Suppose that you can identify your desired destination on the map but cannot actually see it in the field. You can read the UTM position of the destination off the map and then enter it into the GPS memory as a waypoint.

Going back to the Glacier Peak example shown in figure 45, suppose you wish to find the route to the summit of Glacier Peak. From the map, you can see that the summit of Glacier Peak is about halfway between the eastings of 6 40 000 and 6 41 000, so you could estimate the easting as 10 6 40 500 (the zone number in this example is 10). You can also see that the summit is about three-tenths of the way between the northings of 53 30 000 and 53 31 000, so you can estimate the full northing to be 53 30 300N. You can now enter the UTM coordinates of 10 6 40 500E and 53 30 300N into the GPS receiver. (With most receivers, this is done by displaying any previously saved waypoint, and then using up, down, right, and left arrow buttons to replace [edit] the existing numbers with the new ones for the new waypoint.) You can then name the waypoint (e.g., "GLPEAK") and save it. Be sure to read your GPS receiver instruction manual carefully to find the specific directions for creating and saving a waypoint from a map.

Once you have entered your destination into the GPS receiver's memory, give it a couple minutes to acquire a position. Then ask it to GO TO the name of the new waypoint ("GLPEAK" in this example), and the receiver will display the distance and compass bearing from wherever you are to the summit of Glacier Peak. Now set this bearing on your magnetic compass, turn off the GPS receiver and put it away, and follow the compass bearing until you arrive at Glacier Peak.

What if you find yourself off route due to a crevasse or other obstruction? After passing the obstruction, turn on the GPS receiver, acquire a position, and again ask it to GO TO your destination waypoint. The receiver will then provide the new distance and compass bearing to your destination. Set this new bearing on your compass and follow it to your destination.

Problems 29 and 30 in the appendix provide additional practice in using the UTM system.

DATUMS, ZONES, AND BANDS

The *map datum* is a reference that is usually found in the lower left corner of the topographic map. Several different systems are in use: WGS (World Geodetic System) 84, NAD (North American Datum) 1927, NAD 1983, and others. Before using your GPS receiver with a map, find this datum on your map, go to the receiver's setup screen, and set the datum to agree with your map. Figure 44 shows the lower left-hand corner of the map for Glacier Peak. The 1927 North American Datum is clearly identified as the datum. Most GPS receivers have a default datum of WGS84, whereas most USGS topographic maps use the NAD27 datum. The difference between these two datums can be as much as a thousand feet (hundreds of meters). It is therefore essential to set your GPS receiver datum to be in agreement with the datum for the map you are using.

The *UTM zone* can usually be found on maps that include UTM lines or grid ticks (see fig. 44, for zone 10). There are sixty UTM zones around the world, and each is 6° wide. Zone 1 is for the area from 180° W to 174° W, and its zone meridian (centerline) is 177° W. Zone 2 is to the east of zone 1: from 174° W to 168° W, with a zone meridian of 171° W. From this you should be able to figure out the zone of any longitude. The centerline of each zone is numbered 5 00 000mE. This centerline is the reference line for east-west positions (eastings).

Some GPS receivers use a *latitude band* with UTM to indicate position relative to the equator. This system divides the earth into 8-degree-wide latitude bands from 80° S latitude to 84° N latitude (the northernmost band being a bit wider than the others). The bands are lettered from south to north, according to the following table:

LATITUDE BANDS AND LATITUDE RANGES

Lat. Band	Lat. Range	Lat. Band	Lat. Range
C	72-80 South	N	0-8 North
D	64-72 South	P	8-16 North
E	56-64 South	Q	16-24 North
F	48-56 South	R	24-32 North
G	40-48 South	S	32-40 North
H	32-40 South	T	40-48 North
J	24-32 South	U	48-56 North
K	16-24 South	V	56-64 North
L	8-16 South	W	64-72 North
M	0-8 South	X	72-84 North

If the latitude band is used, the letter for that band is placed immediately after the zone number. Some GPS receivers require using such a latitude band. Others merely ask you to indicate which hemisphere you are in, north or south.

Due to distortion of the UTM grid lines near the poles, UTM is not defined north of 84° N or south of 80° S latitude. The area covered by UTM includes most of the world, except Antarctica and arctic regions north of Alaska's north coast. In those areas you can use latitude and longitude, or the Universal Polar Stereographic (UPS) grid instead.

LIMITATIONS OF GPS RECEIVERS

The GPS receiver is not a substitute for a map and compass and the ability to use them. Most GPS receivers cannot determine direction, so you still need a compass to use GPS in the wilderness. Most GPS receivers can tell you the straight-line route from one point to another, but they have no way of knowing if there is a river, a lake, or a cliff along this route. For this reason, you still must have a topographic map with you, even if you also have a GPS receiver.

Some of the more expensive GPS receivers contain built-in maps and can accept topographic maps downloaded from your computer. These receivers can show your position directly on the screen of your receiver. While this is a very useful feature, it does not replace the need for conventional maps, because you still need to be able to view the big picture of the route, as well as avoid total dependence on the GPS receiver.

Some high-end GPS receivers also contain built-in electronic compasses. Using such an instrument eliminates the need to set the correct course bearing on your magnetic compass. You can then conceivably do all your navigating using only your GPS receiver. Even with such a receiver, however, you still need to carry a magnetic compass, in case the GPS receiver does not work.

Most GPS receivers will not work at temperatures much below freezing, and battery life is limited depending on the model and the type of batteries used.

GPS receivers must track signals from at least four satellites in order to provide trustworthy position information, but if the satellite signals are blocked by heavy forest cover, cliffs, or canyons, this is often not possible. When a GPS receiver is not able to pick up signals from the four satellites it needs in order to provide a three-dimensional position, it sacrifices altitude information in favor of horizontal position. Some receivers indicate that this is happening by displaying a "2D" message or icon to tell you that it is operating in a two-dimensional mode. Other receivers may merely display a "frozen" altitude display if this occurs. In either case, always note whether you are getting a two-dimensional position. If so, then be aware of the fact that the GPS receiver's horizontal position may be significantly in error as well, particularly if you are thousands of feet or meters above sea level. Under such less-than-ideal conditions, horizontal position errors of up to 1000 feet (hundreds of meters) are possible.

Because of the slight possibility that a GPS receiver might have a position error, it is wise to exercise some caution before using or saving a waypoint. For example, suppose you are in a parking lot at a trailhead and you acquire a GPS position. This will be an important waypoint, since you will certainly want to get back to this point at the end of your trek. Instead of just mindlessly saving this position, you should first observe the UTM coordinates indicated on the screen of the receiver and compare them to the map. These coordinates should indicate a position very close to your location. Also, observe the elevation indicated on the GPS receiver screen, and compare it with that shown on your map. Again, they should agree closely. Any significant difference between either your position or your altitude and that shown on the GPS receiver should alert you to the possibility that you might have an erroneous GPS position, perhaps due to signal reflections off cliffs, cars, or other structures, or perhaps due to some atmospheric disturbance. In this case, wait a few minutes or walk a few yards away and try again. Do not save any important waypoint until you have verified that it is in reasonable agreement with your position as shown on the map.

A truly important waypoint should be a 3D position, since a 2D position can have errors of up to hundreds of meters. Some receivers even warn you of this when you try to save (mark) a waypoint; one model of GPS receiver displays a statement, "Warning—This is a 2D FIX! Continue with Mark?" If this occurs, it is best to move to a location with better visibility and wait for a 3D position to be obtained.

GPS receivers are marvelous devices, and using them can significantly aid wilderness navigation. Keep in mind, however, that they are not absolutely foolproof, and that topography, forest cover, battery life, electronic failure, and cold temperatures can cause problems in their use. A GPS receiver cannot replace conventional map and compass techniques. Compasses work at temperatures well below zero, require no batteries, and are so simple that there is very little that can go wrong with them. In addition, compasses are so lightweight and inexpensive that every party member can carry one. They are easy to operate and understand, and they function in even the thickest of forests. The map and compass remain the cornerstones of navigation and wilderness routefinding.

Wilderness Routefinding

Routefinding begins at home. Before heading out the door, you need to know not only the name of your wilderness destination but also a great deal about how to get there and back. This information is accessible to anyone who takes the time to seek it out, from guidebooks and maps and from people who have been there.

Any off-trail trip requires a *route plan*, that is, a well thought-out plan for how the group will navigate to its destination and back.

Prepare for each trip as if you were going to lead it, even if you are not. Each person in the group needs to know wilderness navigation and must keep track of where the party has been, where it is, and where it is going. In case of an emergency, each party member must be able to get back, alone. Each member of the party must therefore know and understand the route plan.

Guidebooks provide critical information, such as a description of the route, the estimated time necessary to complete it, elevation gain, distance, and so forth. Travelers who have previously made the trip may be able to tell you about landmarks, hazards, and routefinding hassles. Useful details are packed into maps of all sorts: Forest Service, road, aerial, sketch, and topographic. For a trip into an area that is particularly unfamiliar to you, more preparation is needed. This might include scouting into the area, observations from distant vantage points, or a study of aerial photographs.

If the route comes from a guidebook or from a description provided by another person, plot it out on the topographic map you will be carrying, noting trail junctions and other important points. It can help to highlight the route with a yellow felt-tip marking pen, which does not obliterate map features. Additional maps or route descriptions marked with notes on any more up-to-date information should be taken, along with the topographic map. In selecting the route consider a host of factors including the season, weather conditions, the abilities of party members, and the equipment available.

Before you have even shouldered your pack, you should have a mental image of the route. From experience and from all the sources of information about the trip, you should know how to make the terrain work in your favor. A rock slide area can be a feasible route, providing that you watch for new rockfall. One problem in planning your route, however, is that a rock slide area may look the same on a map as an avalanche gully, which can be an avalanche hazard in winter and spring and choked with brush in summer and fall. If your information sources are not helpful, only a firsthand look will clear up this question.

The most straightforward return route is often the same as the route going in. To minimize the possibility of getting off track, it is usually best to return by the same route as on the way to your objective. If you plan to come back a different way, then that route also needs careful advance preparation.

You should not let outdated information ruin your trip. Check beforehand with the appropriate agencies about roads and trails, especially closures, and also about off-trail routes, regulations, permits, and camping requirements.

ON THE TRAIL

When following trails be sure to make note of all trail junctions. Some are indistinct, unmarked, or obscure. Others, though marked with signs, are easy to miss if you are in a hurry or not paying close attention. When following a good trail through nondescript territory, it is easy to get into a form of mental autopilot, in which you just keep on walking without taking much note of features you are passing. In such conditions, it is easy to miss trail junctions and wander off onto the wrong trail. Try to avoid this by remaining alert to your surroundings and always searching for trail junctions and other noteworthy features.

At clearings in the forest, trail junctions, stream crossings, passes, and other locations, locate your position on the map. Be observant of the topography that you pass. For example, you may see a ridge or a gully coming down a mountainside, and you can glance at your map to note that you are passing such a feature. In addition to helping you to keep track of your position, this practice will eventually make you an expert map reader.

When traveling in a group, it is easy to get spread out along the trail, since it is seldom that everyone in a party will walk at the same pace. However, this occasionally leads to people getting separated from the rest of the group and sometimes getting lost. For this reason, it is critically important to stop and wait for stragglers from time to time—at all trail junctions and other places where it might be possible for someone to go astray. If you come to a place where the trail becomes indistinct or otherwise hard to follow, it is essential to stop and wait for all members of the party to catch up. At the beginning of a hike and at various places along the way, the leader should instruct everybody to stop and wait at certain bridges, trail junctions, or other obvious places until the whole group catches up.

When the trail becomes lost in snow, blowdown, or overgrown brush, there are ways to find and stay on track other than just following a well-beaten trail. One way is to look for *tree blazes*—slashes, usually made by an ax, normally about 6 feet or so above ground level. Another telltale sign are the *prunings* that are occasionally visible, where tree limbs have been cut during trail maintenance operations. If neither of these helps you to stay on the trail, ask yourself, "If I were a trail, where would I be?" Trail builders usually locate trails on the easiest terrain, with a minimum of ups and downs, and with the least amount of effort. Remembering this may help you to relocate the trail. If you do lose the trail in brush, woods, or snow, then you should immediately stop, retrace your steps, and locate the last known trail position. It is often tempting to keep pressing on, with the notion that the trail will eventually emerge. But this is rarely the case. Go back and find the trail and then start the process of finding the true route to your destination, whether back on the original trail, or by some other route.

Even if the trail is muddy or full of puddles, it is strongly recommended that you stay on the trail, walking right through the puddles, even if it means getting your feet wet. (The inconvenience of this practice is lessened by wearing appropriate footwear: good, solid, waterproofed boots that will not soak through when you walk through water.) Walking off the trail to find dry spots eventually creates multiple parallel paths and causes a severe human impact on the wilderness. In addition, be careful not to damage trailside vegetation—for example, take rest stops at places with rocks or logs, or at open bare areas, rather than at places where you might damage trailside vegetation.

IN THE FOREST

The moment you step off the road or trail and enter the forest, remind yourself that you are leaving your handrail, and you need to look for another one. The new handrail could be a topographic feature, such as a ridge, gully, or stream. In the total absence of real, physical hand-rails, you can conceivably follow an invisible abstract handrail, such as a contour line (by keeping level, neither gaining nor losing elevation) or a compass bearing. If you do this, be sure to make a note of the elevation or bearing that you are following. Never merely wander off into the woods with no clear idea of the direction in which you are headed. You will also need a new baseline; this might be the road or trail that was your previous handrail.

It is best to try to follow topographic features when choosing a route in the forest. To avoid heavy brush, try to follow ridges and dense, old-growth timber, if you can find it. Gullies, watercourses, and second growth may be choked with lush, difficult vegetation. You may encounter remnants of trails from time to time. If so, take advantage of them, since doing so may save you time and energy. But keep in mind that the destination of such a trail may well be different from yours. If the trail starts to deviate too much from your intended direction-of-travel, be prepared to leave it and head back to off-trail travel.

It may sound self-evident and trite, but you should always remember that if you know where you are, you are not lost. So always keep track of your position using topography, time, vegetation, elevation, and any other means at your disposal. Perhaps you headed off into the woods at a bearing of 250° for an hour, until you reached an elevation of 3500 feet as indicated on your altimeter. Then you traversed level terrain at a bearing of 310° in open terrain. And then you ascended a forested ridge until you reached a broad bench at 4800 feet. Be sure to consult the map at frequent intervals to find each topographic feature that you encounter. Record your route in your notebook or on your map. The route will look entirely different on your return, but with the aid of your map, compass, notebook, and perhaps your altimeter, you should be able to get back to your starting point without difficulty.

Mark the route if necessary. When traveling in the forest, it is particularly unlikely that you will follow exactly the same path on your return as on your way in, unless the topography of the area is very distinct. For this reason, it is essential to use biodegradable markers such as toilet paper, which deteriorates without leaving a trace.

If you have a GPS receiver, take the time at the start of your trek to establish a waypoint or landmark. This may be possible at the road where you leave your car. If not, then at least read the UTM coordinates off the map and enter this location as a starting point. Later, if necessary, you can establish a new position and ask the receiver to tell you the compass bearing to your starting point.

Remember to keep your map and compass handy as you travel in the forest. If you carry them in your pack, you will not use them as often as you should, since you will not want to stop frequently to remove your pack. If the route is difficult, with brush, fallen trees, or other obstacles to climb over and under, it is especially important that you not carry your compass with its lanyard around your neck, due to safety concerns. Your pocket is a far better place for it.

Routefinding in a Snowy Forest

Enjoying the wilderness in the early spring or late fall can be a wonderful experience. The air is crisp and cold. Snow covers the forest floor. The bugs are gone, as are the majority of travelers. However, there is one distinct disadvantage to traveling through a forest with snow obscuring the trail: the routefinding can be extremely challenging. With snow over the trail and landmarks and compass bearing objects obscured by forest, the route can be difficult to follow. Wands are very hard to follow in a forest. Further, some GPS receivers will not work well in the forest. The map and altimeter may be your best tools.

Begin honing your skills by traveling on snow-covered trails with which you are familiar. When en route, continually ask yourself where you would be if you were a trail. The moment that you are in unfamiliar terrain, retrace your route to a point at which you are familiar. If you know the direction to your destination then blaze your own trail, but do not expect that your tracks will be recognizable for the return. You may need to find a new and better route for the return. Keep an eye out for trail markers, trail signage, blazes in trees, and significant landmarks on which to take compass bearings. Look for old fallen logs that trail crews have sawed apart for the trail byway. Slow your pace and be diligent. Take existing footprints with a grain of salt. They are just another clue as to where the route may go. Always assume that the travelers who made the existing footprints were lost, until you prove otherwise. Reorient yourself with the smallest sign of a trail—a bridge, a trail marker, or other landmark—and, most importantly, routefind with an open mind.

IN ALPINE AREAS

Many of the same suggestions offered above for forests also apply to alpine areas. First, find and follow a route using natural topographic features wherever possible. You can use ridges, gullies, streams, and other readily identifiable features as handrails. Even if the route appears to be obvious, pause now and then to look at the map and find your location, and observe the topographic features that you are using on your route. The sudden arrival of clouds may turn an obvious route into a challenging navigational problem. Mark your route on the map in pencil, perhaps even noting the time of arrival at various places along the route. Remember that you should be able to identify your position on the map as closely as possible at any point of your trip.

If you must deviate from natural topographic features, then use your compass to find the bearing that you will be following on the next leg of your trip. Make a note of this bearing in your notebook or on the map. If you have an altimeter, look at it often and follow your progress on the map. Ask yourself frequently what you would do if fog or clouds suddenly came in and obscured your view of the return route. How would you recognize key points at which you need to make crucial route changes? Should you be marking the route at such places?

In selecting the route, try to minimize the impact of your party on the terrain. Many alpine areas are particularly fragile. Some delicate woody plants, such as heather, grow only a fraction of an inch (a few millimeters) each season, and a few thoughtless footprints may wipe out an entire season's growth. If there is any trail at all, use it to minimize your impact. In the absence of a trail, try to stick to rocks, scree, talus, or snow to avoid stomping on fragile vegetation. If you must travel over alpine growth, spread out your party to disperse your impact as much as possible.

Open alpine areas are excellent places to use GPS receivers. At every rest stop, and at important route changes, take the opportunity to turn on your receiver and obtain a satellite fix. Save these locations as waypoints. In the event that you wander off route, you may be able to acquire a new position fix. Then your receiver will be able to tell you the bearing to any of your previously established waypoints.

ON SNOW

Always be aware of potential avalanche conditions. If a slope has snow on it, then it has the possibility of sliding, often with deadly results. Slopes with a grade of about 45 percent to 170 percent (an angle of $25°$ to $60°$) have a high likelihood of sliding, so always be aware of the grade of the slope—and not just the slope you are on, but also the slope above you. The most extreme hazard occurs when the slope grade is about 60 percent to 100 percent—an angle of $30°$ to $45°$—so be particularly wary on slopes in this range. (Chapter 6 includes techniques for measuring the grade of a slope on a map, and chapter 7 explains the use of the clinometer for measuring the actual angle of a slope.)

Routefinding on snow is usually straightforward. One advantage of traveling on snow is that wilderness travelers can pick their own route. The best route is usually that which follows the path of least resistance. Take the route that seems to make sense. Many times you can see your destination, and the route is straightforward. The shortest distance between two points is a straight line. Sometimes, however, the direct route is too steep for the party to ascend comfortably. This is where switchbacking comes in, just as on trails that gain elevation quickly. It may be beneficial for the party to make a few deliberate switchbacks to gain altitude instead of wearing out the party by attacking the slope head-on. Remember, while making your steps, kick them in as if you were making them for the party member with the shortest stride. It is easy for the long-strided individual to take shorter steps but difficult for the shorter-strided individual to make longer steps.

Many times you can follow previous bootprints in the snow to find the proper route. Even if bootprints are several days old, an observant navigator can sometimes pick them out from sun cups and still follow the route. Vague bootprints will sometimes have a uniform indentation and may have a distinct, subtle ring of dust in them. But it is still your responsibility to know your approximate location and direction at all times. A wilderness navigator who uses the excuse "It's not my fault that we're lost—I was following tracks!" needs to read this book again before venturing out on another trek.

Following a route that has been put in on a snowfield is often academic: simply follow the bootprints. But prints are rarely permanent and can degrade quickly under some conditions. Wind and newly fallen snow can obliterate tracks, sometimes only a few seconds after they are created. The sun, especially at higher altitudes, can also erase tracks. This can be particularly surprising on a summer day when you thought that your descent following your tracks would be a piece of cake, only to find on your return trip that your footprints have melted out and have become intermingled with existing sun cups. Fortunately for the wilderness traveler, with a little homework and a few navigational tools you will be able to find your way back.

The best tools for routefinding on snow are the map and compass. By taking bearings on an intermediate objective, such as a pass or a rock outcropping, you can navigate toward that objective even if clouds move in. If you write down those compass bearings, then on the return trip you can easily follow the back bearings for each consecutive leg and make it back. Remember though, if you have not done your homework and written down the bearings when you could see where to go, and then the clouds roll in and your footprints are obliterated, you may be in trouble. It may sound obvious, but you must use your map and compass (and pencil) when you can see the route to the destination so that when clouds obscure the route on the return, you can still find your way back.

Another tool for routefinding on snow is the altimeter. The clouds have rolled in, and you press on until reaching what you hope is the summit. But a quick check of the altimeter shows that you are 700 feet lower than the printed summit on the map (assuming a stable barometric pressure). A look at the map shows a false summit 500 feet lower than the true summit. It is likely that you have not quite made it yet.

Consider this situation: You come down from the summit but lose the descent route in the clouds. Your bootprints are gone and you have no wands. You remember that your camp is located at an elevation of 6500 feet. You descend to 6500 feet, as indicated on your altimeter, and your camp is nowhere to be seen. By traversing the slope, maintaining your elevation, you may eventually run into your camp. This technique is imperfect at best, since your altimeter reading may be inaccurate due to changing weather conditions.

A GPS receiver can also be used on snow and in whiteouts. The GPS receiver can give you a pretty good idea of where you are, and where to go, but only if you have set the proper waypoints. By setting waypoints and entering important positions, such as the location of your camp, the receiver can guide you to your objective and back. On long trips when conserving battery power is a concern, you can obtain the proper bearing to your destination from the GPS receiver, set the bearing on your compass, and then follow it using your compass. If being a few dozen feet away from your intended line of travel is not a problem, then the GPS receiver will suit your needs. However, GPS accuracy is not adequate for you to bury a cache of food on a featureless snow slope, save the coordinates, leave for a week, and expect to find the cache again without a wand or other visible marker.

WANDS

You may occasionally have difficulty retracing your ascent route when on an indistinct snowfield where your bootprints are obliterated by wind, sun, or new snow. In this case, a dependable way to follow your ascent route is to follow tall, thin stakes called wands. Think of a set of wands as a portable handrail that you place on the ascent. Most people make their own wands out of 3-foot green bamboo sticks purchased at any gardening store. To make the wands more visible, cut a 6-inch piece of brightly colored duct tape and make a flag at the top of the stick by folding the duct tape back over itself (fig. 46). Wands can be carried behind the compression straps of your pack, where you can reach them for easy placement without removing your pack.

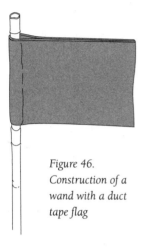

Figure 46. Construction of a wand with a duct tape flag

Placement of Wands

Wands are placed with the descent in mind. Place wands where they will be visible on the return trip. It is always better to place the wand on the top of a small rise rather than in a hollow. Beware of background features, such as rocks or trees, that can cause the wand to blend in with its surroundings. Your wands should be as easy as possible to spot and follow. One helpful trick is to angle the wand slightly toward the previously placed wand. On your return, if you cannot see the next wand, you will have a pretty good idea of the direction to it. If you still cannot see the next wand, then have the party wait at the last wand and cautiously search for the next wand, always remaining in sight or within shouting distance of the rest of the party. Wait until you find the wand, and then proceed to the next wand. It is all too easy for a party to rush down an indistinct snow slope and lose the wands under poor conditions. Once lost, it can be difficult to find the wanded trail again.

If the party is roped up, then a good rule of thumb is to place the wands no farther apart than the combined length of the rope teams. If the terrain does not warrant roping up, then the safety margin must be increased and the wands placed so that you can see at least one and preferably a second wand from each successive wand. It is easiest to find successive wands if they are placed at approximately equal intervals, so that you know where and when to look for them. This might require counting paces between wands to space them at predictable intervals.

If you find that you are running out of wands, then try to supplement the wands you have by using natural terrain features. Perhaps you can place a few wands at regular intervals on an indistinct snowfield until reaching a distinct ridgeline. Then you can follow the ridgeline without placing any wands until its end. At this point you may elect to build a small temporary cairn to mark the route. Another way to conserve wands is to set one wand in a good spot then take a compass bearing toward your previous wand and place a second wand about a foot from the last one, with the wands lined up to point toward the previous one. To follow the course back simply take the compass bearing that the two wands create and follow that bearing to the previous wand(s). In this way you can place pairs of wands farther apart than single wands.

The party should always carry enough wands to make it to the destination. The number of wands depends greatly on the length and complexity of the route. It is not uncommon for a party to carry one hundred wands for a long route. If you are in a party of four, that is only twenty-five wands per person.

Wands left behind are considered litter. Always be sure to remove all your wands on the descent. Never remove someone else's wands, as they are depending on them for their descent. If you encounter someone else's wand that has melted out of the snow and has fallen over, place it upright again. Do not expect to follow somebody else's wands. They may remove them on the descent ahead of you, leaving you stranded. You and your party should be responsible for getting to and from your destination using your own resources.

It is possible that you may run out of wands before you reach your destination. Perhaps the conditions warrant more wands then you had anticipated. If this is the case, the party must decide a proper course of action. Perhaps you can use another form of navigation, such as taking a bearing from the last placed wand toward your known destination. Careful study of the map or an altimeter reading may help. Perhaps a GPS receiver can give some clues. (Remember that the GPS receiver is not a panacea. It may not be accurate enough to indicate the position of your last placed wand.) Standing at the last placed wand in a whiteout close to your destination can be disheartening. In this situation you must be very careful. You have walked out onto the end of the proverbial plank. The prudent decision may be to follow your wands back down and try again some other day, and bring more wands next time!

ON GLACIERS

As the route ascends high above tree line and onto snowfields, the routefinding becomes easier. Snow covers the talus and protects the fragile meadows. But a new hazard may be lurking underneath: crevasses. Many times there is a traditional roping up point that divides the nontechnical ascent from the technical. At other times, in the absence of a terminal or lateral moraine, and especially in early season, it may be difficult to determine exactly where the snowfield ends and the glacier begins. Triangulate your position on the map. Does your triangulation show that you are you within a white area with a dashed blue boundary line and blue contour lines? Then you may have crossed onto a glacier. *Rope up for all glacier travel!* This next section assumes that you are tied in to the climbing rope.

The tools and techniques used for routefinding on snow can be used on glaciers as well. You will have two primary concerns while traveling on glaciers. One is that the route is as efficient as possible, as straight a line as the team can handle, leading to your objective. The second, and sometimes contradictory concern, is that the route avoids objective hazards, such as major icefall areas, cornices, and avalanche slopes, and travels over as few crevasses as possible.

Generally, an established route across a glacier follows a line that crosses the fewest crevasses. Many times, just as on snow, a previous route can be followed. Often, on popular glacier routes, the route will be a well-paved "trail" along the glacier surface. Sometimes it is so good that it forms a veritable pathway, making an otherwise steep and tricky traverse an easy walk.

Occasionally, if the route is old or if it is late in the season, it will end at a gaping crevasse, the sign of a collapsed snow bridge. A new route will have to be made over or around the crevasse in order to continue. Always be prepared to put in the route yourself.

Crevasses tend to be most plentiful around turns and obstructions and near the sides of the glacier. Often, the center of the glacier may have a more homogeneous bedrock base and thus fewer, albeit deeper crevasses. Crevasses tend to form in groups with their attitude perpendicular to the direction of glacier flow.

Sometimes, if there is a crevasse that has just begun to show itself, a previous party may have placed two wands together forming an **X**. This is a warning to steer clear—a crevasse is probably looming underneath the snow surface. The proper way to travel around a known crevasse is to steer wide around it; this is called an *end-run*. Oftentimes on a glacier, a crevasse will exist beneath an otherwise unexplained dip in the snow surface. As you approach, probe the snow deeply with your ice ax, and look through the hole to see if there is a crevasse. Step wide over the dip. Tread lightly and step over anything that you suspect may be a crevasse. Remember, too, that if you are putting in the route then it is likely that many more will follow your path, perhaps even in your very footsteps. You should craft a route that is manageable for all wilderness travelers, not just for the athletic.

While ascending, keep in mind the descent path. If you jump over a crevasse with uneven side walls, be sure that you will be able to jump over it again on the descent. Additionally, you want your route to last for several days, not hours, and summertime glacier surface melt is often significant, up to several inches per day. For this reason it is best to make long end runs and cross on thick snow bridges.

Most prudent summit attempts on glacier routes are begun a few hours before the coolest part of the day. With a cold air temperature, snow bridges are firmer and the glacier surface is more likely to be frozen over, making for smooth cramponing, instead of slushy postholing. Time your start so that your descent is completed well before the heat of the day. It is common for summit teams to leave high camp between midnight and four o'clock in the morning, summit, and return to high camp before noon.

With a large party on an unblazed glacier route, it may be advantageous to send a scouting party ahead to put in the route. Alternatively, a small side trip might yield an excellent vantage point from which to view the glacier from a distance. At such a point, you may more easily see the big picture of where the route should be heading, as well as any major obstacles such as icefalls that must be avoided.

MOATS AND BERGSCHRUNDS

The areas between moving snow and ice masses and stationary features, such as rock ridges, moraines and summit ice caps are often defined by the existence of a moat or bergschrund.

Moats form when rock, radiated by the sun, warms and melts the snow near it. Moats can be dozens of feet deep and can be difficult to see from below. Moats have a propensity to swallow up ankles, legs, and unsecured equipment. If you are on a snow surface, approaching a rock feature, always assume that a moat is lurking. As you approach the rock, probe the snow with your ice ax and look through the hole to see if the rock is visible. Step wide over the gap. It may be advantageous to cross the precipice laterally or even downhill to get a wider stride.

Bergschrunds commonly occur high on a mountain face. They are formed when the moving ice or snow mass separates from the summit ice or rock. Early in the season they may be filled in with snow and crossing them may be academic; you may not even notice them. But later in the season they can present challenging routefinding problems. Sometimes a snow bridge may cross a bergschrund. Other times the safest course is to steer wide around them, perhaps even climbing on the smooth rock at its end. Deep and wide bergschrunds can present such a significant routefinding obstacle that the team may have to turn back. There is not always a way around them.

THE BOOTPRINT

Every bootprint tells a story. Bootprints can tell you a lot about who and when someone has walked in the path before you. As you travel, pay attention to who is in front of you and what type of prints they are leaving. Pay attention to the size of the print, the shape of the sole, the style of the tread pattern, the depth of the print, and the direction of the print. Was the person who left those prints tall or short? Were they wearing a big, heavy pack, causing deep prints? Or were they wearing tennis shoes? Do you know what your own bootprint looks like? Could you follow it back after other people have made new prints on top of it?

How can you tell if you are the first travelers of the day on any particular route? Well, if the only prints that you see are facing you and look like they may have been made the previous day, then chances are that you are the only ones up there.

How far ahead is the next person? In the forest, if the tracks that you are following are filling in with water from a puddle, then the hiker is right around the corner. If the prints have fir needles or leaves on them, then they are older. If the tracks in the mud are drying and becoming less defined, then the party must be at least a few hours ahead of you.

How are your teammates' energy levels doing? If someone is ahead of you and wearing crampons, then you can make very specific observations about their gait. Are there two long parallel streaks leading to the rear crampon marks? This may indicate a party member who is getting tired. The important point here is to be aware. Use all the information that is available, not just what is obvious.

Once, a large group was ascending a trail. One member had to stop to make a clothing adjustment. He told everyone to continue on. One other experienced party member waited with him. The two began to follow after a few minutes. The route began to be obscured by snow, but the tracks from the party ahead were fresh and easy to follow. Then the tracks split into two different directions. Both sets of tracks were made at about the same time. (It was a popular route.) "Which way do we go?" the less experienced man asked. The more experienced man knelt down and carefully examined the two paths, without disturbing them. He reached down and touched some of the prints, testing them and seeing how the snow had formed in the spaces between where the cleats of the boot had left the prints. "They went this way," the experienced man pointed. "How do you know?" the other man asked. The more experienced man explained that he had noticed that the last person in the group that they were following was a woman, who was wearing the same style of boot that he was wearing, only it was about five sizes smaller. The odds of someone else having the same size and style of boot as that woman at that hour on that trail were low. Therefore, they went that way. All they needed to do was to follow those same prints. The two followed the unique prints and after a few minutes they caught up with their group. If the two of them had simply blundered along, unaware of the tracks that they were following, they might have missed their group's turn and might have had to double back after not finding them. But because of experience and awareness, they were able to find their group with little trouble.

Know your own bootprint. And know the bootprints of other members of your party. You may not be able to pick out every step taken along the way, but chances are you will be able to discern between ascending and descending prints, and more importantly, any changes in the prints that you are following.

THE ART OF WILDERNESS ROUTEFINDING

Orientation and navigation are sciences that can be easily mastered by anyone who takes the time, and makes the effort, to learn map reading and the use of the compass and other navigational tools. Practice and time spent on these subjects will enable anyone to become proficient with them. Routefinding is different. It is an art.

Some individuals seem to be born with an innate gift for finding and following a route on trails, through the forest, in alpine regions, and on snow and glaciers. The natural abilities of such people can be greatly enhanced if they thoroughly learn the sciences of orientation and navigation, through mastery of the map, compass, and other tools. Such knowledge can enable a good routefinder to become a great one.

Some other people are not blessed with great natural ability in routefinding. But there is hope for them, too. Through study and practice, they can also become proficient in orientation and navigation. They can even become experts in the use of the map and compass, if they expend the time and effort required to do so. Then, with time and experience, they can acquire much of the art of routefinding, particularly if they travel in the company of good routefinders, observing and learning as they do. Above all, there is no substitute for experience and practice.

We encourage you to reread and study this book carefully, learning the sciences of map reading, compass use, orientation, and navigation, and possibly the use of other navigational tools. But this book is not enough. Repeated practice and considerable experience are necessary to thoroughly develop the skills and acquire the self-confidence that comes with repeated use of the principles described in this book. So go out into the wilderness and put the principles of *Wilderness Navigation* into practice—at first, perhaps, on good trails, then progressing to off-trail travel with ever-increasing routefinding challenges. Eventually, whether you are a natural-born routefinder or not, you can become thoroughly adept at map and compass use and will at least possess the knowledge and experience to avoid getting lost—and recover gracefully from the experience if you ever do get lost. And who knows, someday you might become a great routefinder, able to successfully navigate your way to any destination, solving all problems along the way, and make it back to your starting point with little difficulty or incident—because you planned it that way.

Bibliography

PART 1: BOOKS ON MAPS, COMPASSES, ALTIMETERS, AND GPS

These are only a few of the many books available on the subject matter contained in *Wilderness Navigation*. These particular books are mentioned here because they are sources of some of the information for this book, or simply because they are good books on these subjects. Other fine books on these subjects, many of which are out of print and difficult to purchase, can be found in libraries.

Be Expert with Map and Compass: The Complete Orienteering Handbook, Bjorn Kjellstrom, Collier Books, 1994. Contains useful information on maps, compasses, and their use together, plus information on the sport of orienteering. Latest edition of a classic book on maps and compasses.

GPS Made Easy: Using Global Positioning Systems in the Outdoors, 4th ed., Lawrence Letham, The Mountaineers Books, 2003. Contains useful, practical instructions for using GPS receivers with UTM, latitude and longitude, and the UPS grid at the poles. Contains practical information not found in most GPS receiver instruction manuals (e.g., information on UTM).

The Land Navigation Handbook: The Sierra Club Guide to Map and Compass, W. S. Kals, Sierra Club Books, 1983. Basic, step-by-step instructions for using map and compass with a slightly modified Silva method. Includes direction of the slope, grade measurement, finding north with the stars in both hemispheres, and much more.

Map, Compass and Campfire, a Handbook for the Outdoorsman, Donald E. Ratliff, Binfords & Mort, 1964. Contains detailed information on the section, range, and township coordinate system, plus additional information on maps, compasses, campfires, and survival methods.

Maps and Compasses, 2nd ed., Percy W. Blandford, TAB Books (division of McGraw-Hill, Inc.), 1992. Much detailed information on road maps, topographic maps, nautical charts, map reading, orienteering, compass use, and more.

Staying Found: The Complete Map and Compass Handbook, 3rd ed., June Fleming, The Mountaineers Books, 2001. Orientation and navigation using the method of orienting the map. Also includes finding directions with an analog wristwatch and the sun, aligning your tent to catch the morning sun, navigating with children, and more.

PART 2: BOOKS ON OTHER ASPECTS OF WILDERNESS TRAVEL

These books are recommended to readers of *Wilderness Navigation* because they contain material that is important to all wilderness travelers, such as avalanche safety, first aid and accident response, climbing and scrambling, crevasse rescue, and more.

The ABC's of Avalanche Safety, 3rd ed., E. R. LaChapelle, The Mountaineers Books, 2003. Quintessential text for the backcountry user who expects to encounter avalanche terrain.

Glacier Travel and Crevasse Rescue, 2nd ed., Andy Selters, The Mountaineers Books, 1999.

Leave No Trace Skills and Ethics Series, National Outdoor Leadership School. Separate volumes cover various parts of the United States. For information call 1-800-332-4100.

Medicine for Mountaineering and Other Wilderness Activities, 5th ed., James A. Wilkerson, The Mountaineers Books, 2001. How to prevent and treat injuries and illnesses encountered in the mountain environment.

Mountaineering First Aid: A Guide to Accident Response and First Aid Care, 5th ed., Jan Carline and Martha Lentz, The Mountaineers Books, 2004. Covers specifics of backcountry first aid when 911 is not available. Details the seven steps of accident response.

Mountaineering: The Freedom of the Hills, 7th ed., Steve Cox and Kris Fulsaas, ed., The Mountaineers Books, 2003. The complete book on wilderness travel. From boot selection to aid, ice, and expedition climbing techniques, this is the bible of the mountaineering crowd.

Northwest Mountain Weather: Understanding and Forecasting for the Backcountry User, Jeff Renner, The Mountaineers Books, 1992. Northwest meteorologist explains weather patterns and trends encountered in the mountain environment.

Winning the Avalanche Game, Wasatch Interpretive Association (Salt Lake City, Utah), sixty-minute video, 1993. Informative, realistic, and lively discussion of avalanche terrain, how to minimize danger, and how to use avalanche beacons.

Appendix:
Wilderness Navigation
Practice Problems

All of the problems and questions on each of the following pages are to be done with reference to the map on the facing page. For measuring and plotting bearings on the map, you should assume that the solid vertical lines are aligned with north and south. The answers to all of the problems and questions are given at the end of this appendix.

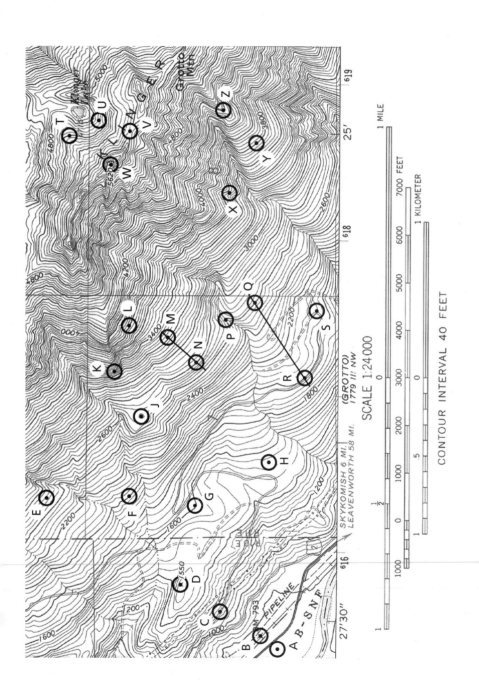

Figure 47. Map to be used with questions 1 through 8.

1. Name the general topographic features depicted at the following points:

A _____ D _____ H _____ K _____ L _____ P _____ U _____

V _____ Z _____

2. What is the straight-line distance from point J to point X?

_____ miles _____ feet _____ meters

3. What is the distance along the road from point C to point S?

_____ miles _____ feet _____ meters

4. What are the elevations, in feet, at each of the following points?

G _____ F _____ E _____ B _____ W _____

5. What is the grade of the slope between points N and M? _____

6. What is the grade of the slope between points R and Q? _____

7. What is the general direction of the slope (fall line) at point Y? _____

8. What is the bearing of the slope (fall line) at point T? _____

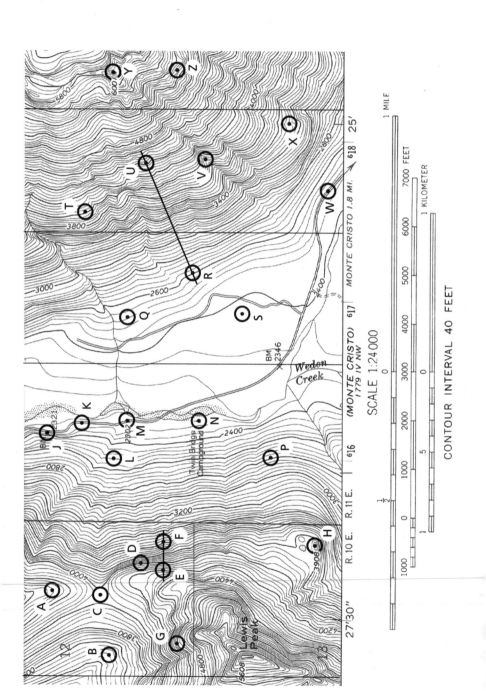

Figure 48. Map to be used with questions 9 through 16.

9. Name the general topographic features depicted at the following points:

A _____ B _____ C _____ D _____ H _____ Q _____ S _____

V _____ Z _____

10. What is the straight-line distance from point J to point N?

_____ miles   _____ feet   _____ meters

11. What is the distance along the road from point K to point W?

_____ miles   _____ feet   _____ meters

12. What are the elevations, in feet, at each of the following points?

P _____ L _____ Y _____ X _____ M _____

13. What is the grade of the slope between points R and U? _____

14. What is the grade of the slope between points E and F? _____

15. What is the general direction of the slope (fall line) at point G? _____

16. What is the bearing of the slope (fall line) at point T? _____

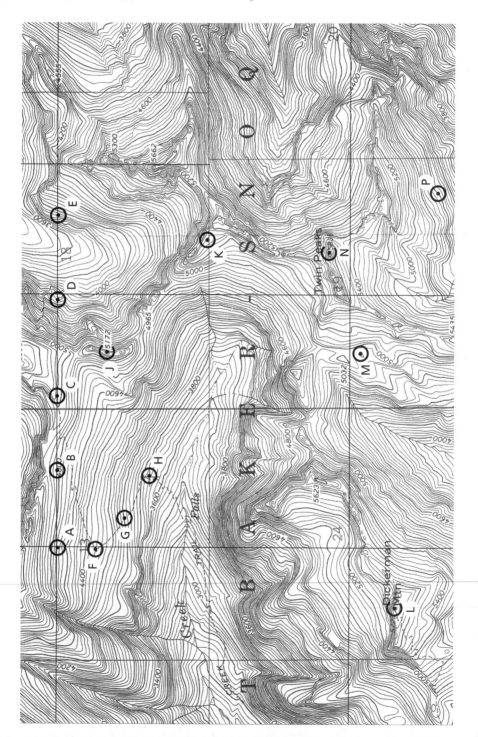

Figure 49. Map to be used with problems 17 through 23.

17. What is the bearing from point P to point M? _____

18. Plot a bearing of 315° from point K. Where does this plotted line intersect the horizontal line at the top of the map? _____

19. You are somewhere on this map, but you do not know exactly where. You take a bearing on the east peak of Twin Peaks (point N) and get 128°. You then take a bearing on Dickerman Mtn. (point L) and get 207°. Where are you? _____

20. You are hiking along the trail in the upper left portion of this map. You wish to find out exactly where you are. You take a bearing on Peak 5172 (point J) and get a bearing of 93°. Where are you? _____

21. You are on the trail in the upper left part of this map. Your altimeter reads 4000 feet. Where are you? _____

22. From the east peak of Twin Peaks (point N), you descend to the northeast. At about what elevation do you expect to encounter a steep cliff? _____

23. From the summit of Peak 5172 (point J), you see a peak and take a bearing on it. You get 185°. What is the approximate elevation of this peak? _____

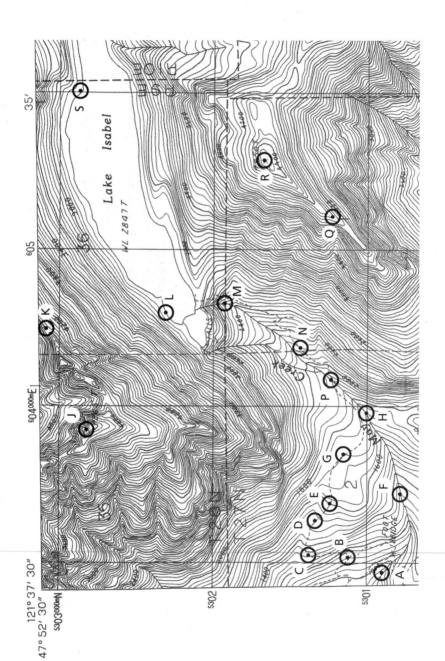

Figure 50. Map to be used with problems 24 through 30.

24. What is the bearing from point S to point R? _____

25. You are along May Creek, but you do not know exactly where. You take a bearing on Peak 4450 (point R) and get 72°. Where are you? (Indicate the letter closest to your position.) _____

26. You take a bearing on Peak 4450 (point R) and get 78°. You take a bearing on Peak 4865 (point J) and get 17°. Where are you? (Indicate the letter closest to your position.) _____

27. You are somewhere along May Creek. Your altimeter shows an elevation of 1320 feet. Where are you? (Indicate the letter closest to your position.) _____

28. Your intended destination is the pass at point K. You do not know your present position. You take a bearing on point R (Peak 4450) and get 159°. You also take a bearing on point J (Peak 4865) and get 271°. What bearing should you follow to get to point K? _____

29. You are in UTM Zone 10. You are at point L, and you turn on your GPS receiver. What is the approximate UTM reading of easting and northing that you should see on the GPS receiver? _____

30. Your intended destination is point Q. You wish to enter this as a waypoint on your GPS receiver. What UTM coordinates would you enter on the receiver? _____

ANSWERS TO PROBLEMS

1. A: Nearly flat area   D: Summit   H: Gentle slope   K: Cliff
   L: Steep slope   P: Gully   U: Bowl (amphitheater)
   V: Saddle or pass   Z: Ridge
2. 0.95 mile, 5000 feet, and 1500 meters (1.5 km)
3. 2.2 miles, 11,600 feet, and 3500 meters (3.5 km)
4. G: 1600 feet   F: 2000 feet   E: 2500 feet   B: 793 feet
   W: 5620 feet
5. Vertical = 400 feet. Horizontal = 800 feet.
   Grade = 400/800 = 0.50, or 50%
6. Vertical = 600 feet. Horizontal = 1900 feet.
   Grade = 600/1900 = 0.32, or 32%
7. General direction of slope (fall line) is southwest. This is the
   direction perpendicular to the contour lines at point Y.
8. Bearing of slope at point T is about 70°.
9. A: Ridge   B: Bowl or amphitheater   C: Saddle or pass
   D: Cliff or very steep slope   H: Peak   Q: Gentle slope
   S: Flat area   V: Gully   Z: Steep slope
10. 0.6 mile, 3200 feet, and 960 meters (0.96 km)
11. 1.5 miles, 7900 feet, and 2400 meters (2.4 km)
12. P: 2800 feet   L: 2520 feet   Y: 6001 feet   X: 3500 feet
    M: 2302 feet
13. Vertical = 4400 - 2600 = 1800 feet. Horizontal = 2500 feet.
    Grade = 1800/2500 = 0.72, or 72% Note that this is the average
    slope between these two points. From 2600 feet to about 3400
    feet, it is gentler than a 72% grade. Between 3400 feet and 4400
    feet it is steeper than a 72% grade.
14. Vertical = 600 feet. Horizontal = 600 feet.
    Grade = 600/600 = 1.00, or 100%
15. General direction of slope (fall line) is northwest. This is the
    direction perpendicular to the contour lines at point G.
16. Bearing of slope at point T is about 240°.
17. 296°
18. Point C
19. Point H, at elevation 3720 feet along the trail, near a switchback
20. Point F
21. Point G
22. 4400 feet
23. 5240 feet
24. 199°
25. Point P, where the trail crosses May Creek at an elevation of
    about 1900 feet

26. Point E on trail
27. Point F
28. 292°
29. 10 6 04 600E; 53 02 300N
30. 10 6 05 200E; 53 01 200N (the latter number is 53 01 240N, rounded to the nearest 100 meters)

Index

adjustable declination 28-30, 36, 88, 91
aiming off 57, 58
Alaska
  USGS maps for 15
  UTM coverage of 106
alpine areas, routefinding in 113, 114
altimeters 92–96, 116
  decision making, use of in 95
  navigation with 95
  orientation with 94, 95
  precision and accuracy 94
  types of 92, 93
  weather prediction, use in 96
angle of slope 74–77, 87, 88, 114
Antarctica, lack of UTM coverage for 106
area position 46, 48–50
avalanche gully 18, 110
avalanche hazard 74, 114
avoiding getting lost 62–68

back bearing 38, 56, 57, 59
barometer 92, 93, 96
baseline 62, 63, 68, 69
base plate 27-30, 39, 40, 44, 88-91
bearings 30–40, 44
  following 33, 34
  measuring 39, 44
  plotting 39, 40, 44

taking 31, 32, 44
bench mark (BM) 22
bergschrunds 120
bivouac 68
blazes 111
bootprints 115, 116, 121, 122
"boxing" the needle 31, 33, 41, 42, 44, 45, 47, 51, 89

cairns, rock 66, 69
Canada, topographic maps for 25
catch line 63
CGRF 82
checklist, map and compass 43, 44
cellular phones 69
cliffs, signal reflections off (GPS) 107
clinometer 28–30, 87, 88
"cocked hat" technique 50
compass 27–45, 88–91
  brands of 29, 30, 88–91
  information provided by 31–33, 38–41, 87, 88
  parts of 27–29
  tips on use of 42, 43
  types of 27–30, 88–91
contour intervals 15, 18
contour lines 18, 22, 53
  as indication of elevation 18
  interpretation of 18–22
crevasses 21, 118, 119

datum 24, 99, 105
declination 9, 15–17, 29, 30, 34–37, 39, 81–86, 88–91
declination arrow, adjustable 9, 28, 29, 36, 37, 42–45, 88, 89
declination arrow, customized 36, 37
declination change 34, 82–86
declination information, sources of 34, 35, 81–83
degree, definition of 14
dip, compass 45, 86
distance, measurement of 71–73

east declination 34–37
easting 102–104
errors, checking for 42–44, 93, 94, 106, 107
"eyeballing" with UTM 101, 103

fall line 22, 23, 51, 52
forest, routefinding in 111–113
full easting 102
full northing 103

glacier, travel on 118–120
Go To command 99
GPS receivers 24, 97–107
cautions 106–108
dependence on, avoiding 99, 100, 106, 107
features of 97, 98
latitude bands, use of 105, 106
grade See slope
guidebooks 14, 109

handrail 62, 63, 111
headlamp 70

impact (human), minimizing 111, 112, 114
intentional offset 57, 58
intermediate objectives 56, 57

landmark (with GPS) 98
lanyard 28, 29, 113
latitude 14
latitude band 105
line position 46, 47
longitude 14
lost 62–70

magnetic bearing 34–37
magnetic declination 15, 16, 34–37, 81–86
map datum 24, 105
maps 13–26
borders of, importance of 15, 16, 24
colors on 17, 18
contour lines on 18–22
customizing 24
date of 13, 15
declination information on 15, 16
how to carry 24, 25
information in margins of 15, 24, 102
limitations of 23
modifiying 24
scales on 14, 15
topographic 14–22
types of 13, 14
waterproofing 24
where to get 25
map measuring instruments 71, 72
measuring distance 71–73
by counting paces 73
using map scales 71–73

meridian lines 39–41
metric system, advantages
of 72, 73
minute, definition of 14
moats 120

NAD *See map datum*
navigation, definition 10, 54
north, magnetic 15, 34–37
north, true 15, 34–37
north-south lines on maps 17,
39, 40
northing 102–104
notebook, use in monitoring
trip progress 64, 65, 67

obstructions, navigating
around 59, 60, 101
orientation, definition 10, 46
orienting a map 9, 50, 51
orienteering 10

pace, use in measuring
distance 73
point position 46, 47
practicing compass use 41, 42
pretrip preparations 62–64,
109, 110
prunings 111

quadrangle 15
quadrant compasses 89

range 77-80
rear guard 65
revisions of existing maps 18
roamer (also romer) 28, 103,
104
rock slide area, use as a route
18, 110
routefinding, definition 10

route marking 66, 112,
116–118
route plan 63, 64, 67, 109

SA (selective availability) 97
scale, map 14, 15, 71–73,
103, 104
second, definition of 14
section 16, 17, 77–80
series (map) 14, 15
sighting compasses, opti-
cal 41, 90, 91
slope 18, 19, 22, 23, 29,
51–53, 74–77, 87, 88, 96,
114
bearing of 51–53, 96
direction of 22, 23
estimating grade of, from
map 74–77, 114
measuring with clinom-
eter 87, 88, 114
snow, routefinding on
114–116
snowfield, permanent 18
speed of travel 66, 67
sphere of uncertainty
(GPS) 100
sun cups 115
survival 70
sweep, assignment of a 65
switchbacking 115

temperature, effects of on
altimeters 94
Ten Essentials 70
topographic features on
maps 18–22
township 77–80
trails, routefinding on 110,
111
travel speed, estimating 66, 67

trigonometry, use of 76
true bearing 34–37

UPS (Universal Polar Stereo-
graphic) grid 106
U.S. declination map 35
USGS maps 14–22
UTM (Universal Transverse
Mercator) 16, 17, 24, 98,
101–106

Wide Area Augmentation
System (WAAS) 98
wands 116–118

warnings (GPS) 107
watch 67, 92
waypoint (GPS) 98, 99, 104
weather predicting using
altimeter 96
west declination 34–37
WGS See map datum
world declination map 83

zero declination line 34, 35
zone (UTM) meridian 105
zone (UTM) reference
line 105

About the Authors

A longtime member of The Mountaineers, **Bob Burns** has hiked, scrambled, climbed, and snowshoed extensively in Washington, Oregon, and California. He has been teaching classes in the use of map and compass since the late 1970s, not only for Club courses but also for search and rescue groups and local schools. With the assistance of Mike Burns, he is the author of the "Navigation" chapter in *Mountaineering: The Freedom of the Hills,* 7th ed., and he has also written articles on the use of GPS in wilderness travel (with Mike) and on leave-no-trace wilderness practices.

Mike Burns is a rock, ice, and expedition climber who has climbed in the Pacific Northwest, Colorado, Alaska, Canada, Mexico, Argentina, Nepal, Pakistan, and India, including a first ascent in the Himalayas. For the past ten years, he has been an instructor and lecturer on the technical aspects of climbing, including navigation. He has written numerous articles for *The Mountaineer* and *Climbing* magazine. He also served on the revision committee for the seventh edition of *Mountaineering: The Freedom of the Hills,* after being a major contributor to the sixth edition of that book.

THE MOUNTAINEERS, founded in 1906, is a nonprofit outdoor activity and conservation club, whose mission is "to explore, study, preserve, and enjoy the natural beauty of the outdoors . . . . " Based in Seattle, Washington, the club is now the third-largest such organization in the United States, with seven branches throughout Washington State.

The Mountaineers sponsors both classes and year-round outdoor activities in the Pacific Northwest, which include hiking, mountain climbing, ski-touring, snowshoeing, bicycling, camping, kayaking and canoeing, nature study, sailing, and adventure travel. The club's conservation division supports environmental causes through educational activities, sponsoring legislation, and presenting informational programs. All club activities are led by skilled, experienced volunteers, who are dedicated to promoting safe and responsible enjoyment and preservation of the outdoors.

If you would like to participate in these organized outdoor activities or the club's programs, consider a membership in The Mountaineers. For information and an application, write or call The Mountaineers, Club Headquarters, 300 Third Avenue West, Seattle, Washington 98119; 206-284-6310.

The Mountaineers Books, an active, nonprofit publishing program of the club, produces guidebooks, instructional texts, historical works, natural history guides, and works on environmental conservation. All books produced by The Mountaineers fulfill the club's mission.

Send or call for our catalog of more than 450 outdoor titles:

The Mountaineers Books
1001 SW Klickitat Way, Suite 201
Seattle, WA 98134
800-553-4453
mbooks@mountaineers.org
www.mountaineersbooks.org

The Mountaineers Books is proud to be a corporate sponsor of The Leave No Trace Center for Outdoor Ethics, whose mission is to promote and inspire responsible outdoor recreation through education, research, and partnerships. The Leave No Trace program is focused specifically on human-powered (nonmotorized) recreation.

Leave No Trace strives to educate visitors about the nature of their recreational impacts, as well as offer techniques to prevent and minimize such impacts. Leave No Trace is best understood as an educational and ethical program, not as a set of rules and regulations.

For more information, visit www.LNT.org, or call 800-332-4100.

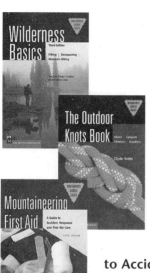

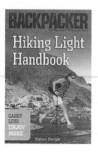